MONSTER HATS

Vanessa Mooncie

MONSTER HATS

15 scary head warmers to knit

First published 2016 by
Guild of Master Craftsman Publications Ltd
Castle Place, 166 High Street, Lewes,
East Sussex BN7 1XU

Text © Vanessa Mooncie, 2016
Copyright in the Work © GMC Publications Ltd, 2016

ISBN 978 1 78494 212 0

A catalogue record for this book is available from the
British Library.

Publisher: Jonathan Bailey
Production Manager: Jim Bulley
Senior Project Editor: Wendy McAngus
Editor: Nicola Hodgson
Pattern checker: Jude Roust
Managing Art Editor: Gilda Pacitti
Art Editor: Rebecca Mothersole
Photographers: Chris Gloag and Rebecca Mothersole
Illustrator: Vanessa Mooncie

Colour origination by GMC Reprographics
Printed and bound in Turkey

Cyclops

Alien

Fiery

Fang

Demon

Fluffball

Troll

Blob

Yeti

Skull

Zombie

Pop-eyes

CONTENTS

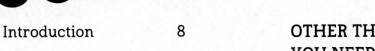

Slug

Fly

Griffin

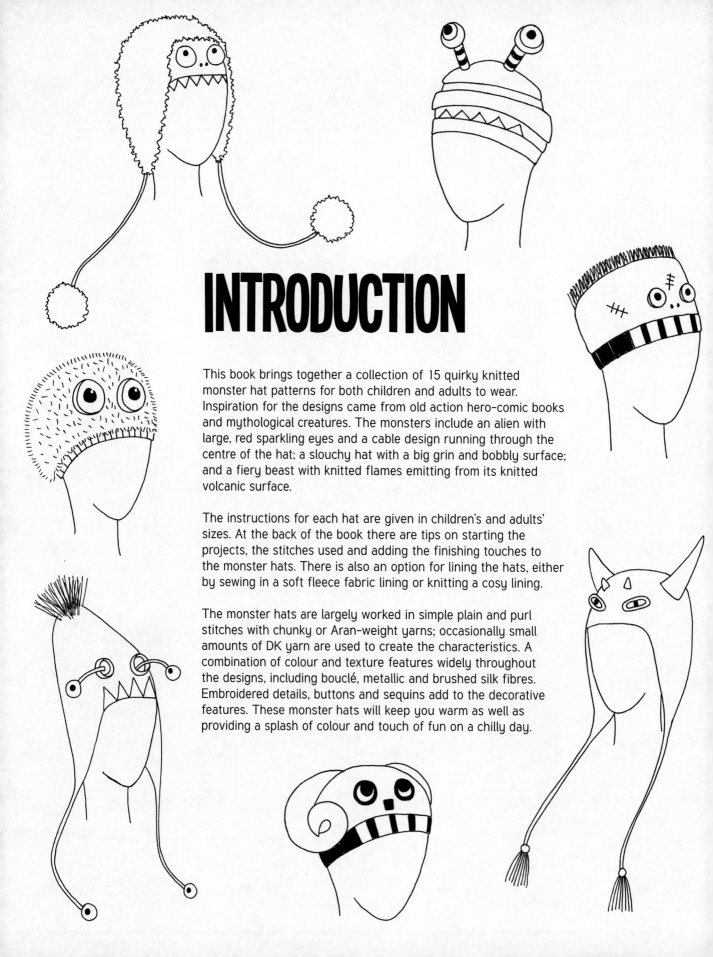

INTRODUCTION

This book brings together a collection of 15 quirky knitted monster hat patterns for both children and adults to wear. Inspiration for the designs came from old action hero-comic books and mythological creatures. The monsters include an alien with large, red sparkling eyes and a cable design running through the centre of the hat; a slouchy hat with a big grin and bobbly surface; and a fiery beast with knitted flames emitting from its knitted volcanic surface.

The instructions for each hat are given in children's and adults' sizes. At the back of the book there are tips on starting the projects, the stitches used and adding the finishing touches to the monster hats. There is also an option for lining the hats, either by sewing in a soft fleece fabric lining or knitting a cosy lining.

The monster hats are largely worked in simple plain and purl stitches with chunky or Aran-weight yarns; occasionally small amounts of DK yarn are used to create the characteristics. A combination of colour and texture features widely throughout the designs, including bouclé, metallic and brushed silk fibres. Embroidered details, buttons and sequins add to the decorative features. These monster hats will keep you warm as well as providing a splash of colour and touch of fun on a chilly day.

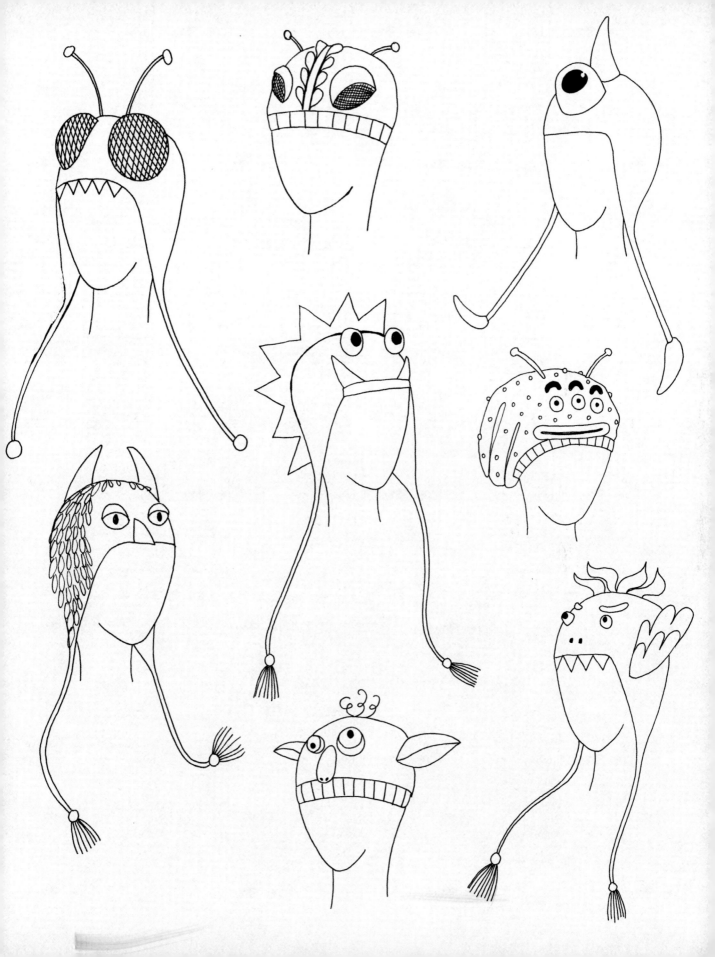

Skull 102

Slug 42

Fly 32

Fiery 36

Blob 96

Demon 82

Fluffball 28

Slug 42

Fly 32

Pop-eyes 54

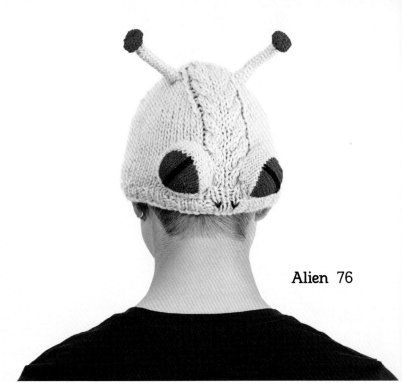

Alien 76

Zombie 72

Pop-eyes 54

Demon 82

Yeti 66

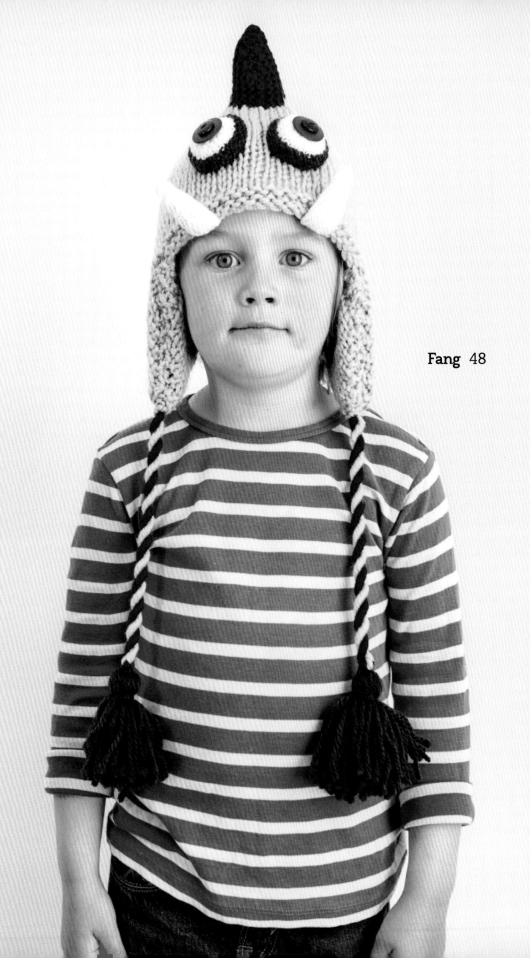

Fang 48

Fly 32

Pop-eyes 54

Griffin 86

Cyclops 60

Troll 106

Demon 82

Zombie 72

Skull 102

Zombie 72

Skull 102

Yeti 66

Demon 82

Cyclops 60

Slug 42

Slug 42

Fluffball 28

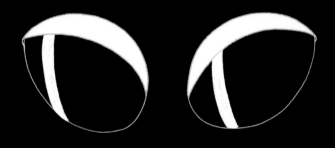

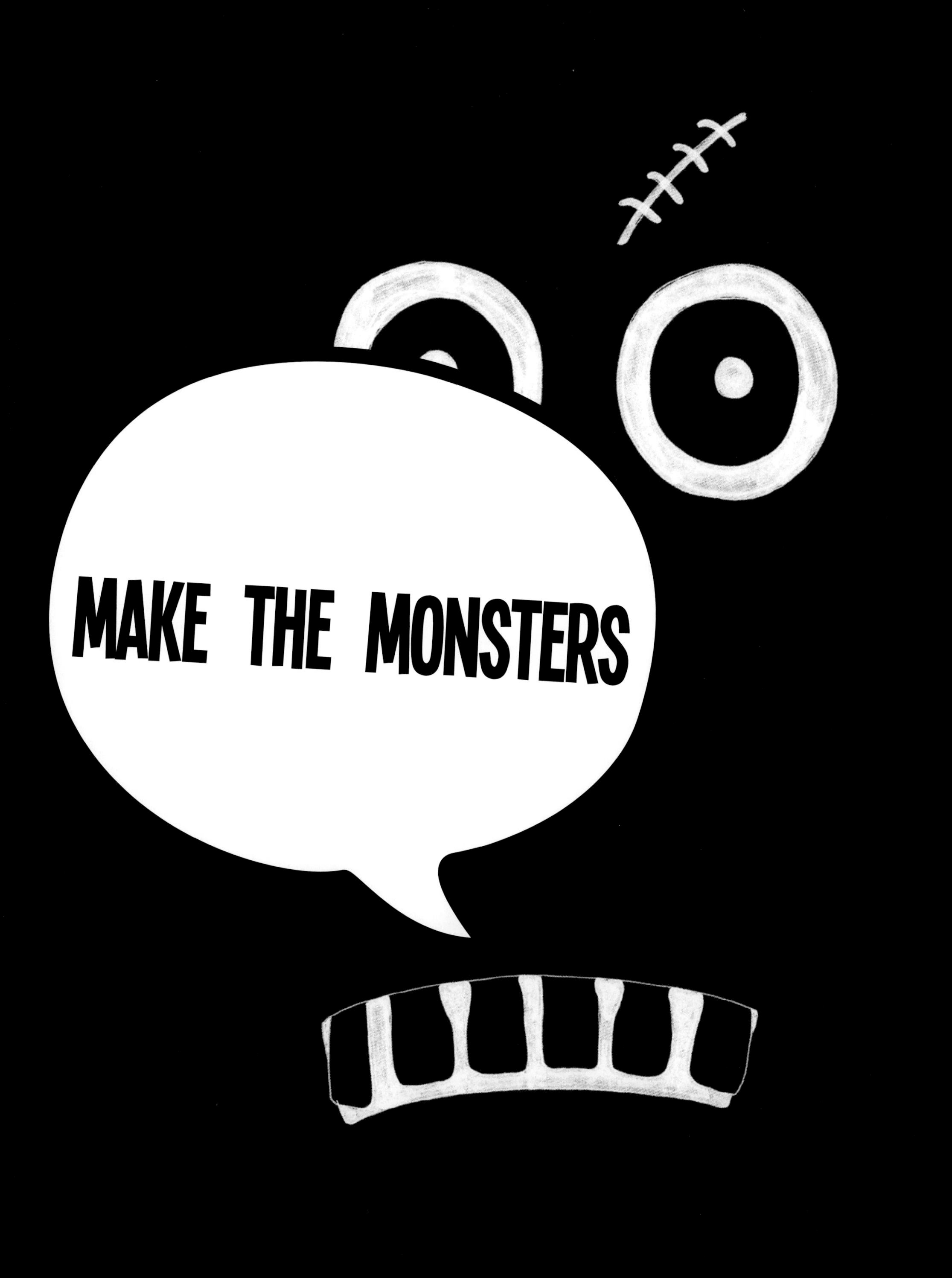
MAKE THE MONSTERS

This furry monster has big eyes peeping through knitted picot lashes. The sparkly yarn, used for the rib and to frame the eyes, contrasts with the wild, fluffy main part of the hat.

materials

- James C Brett Twinkle Fashion DK, 96% acrylic, 4% polyester (328yd/300m per 100g ball): 1[1] ball in TK24 Burgundy (A)
- James C Brett Faux Fur Chunky, 90% nylon, 10% polyester (98yd/90m per 100g ball): 1[1] ball in H6 Burgundy/White (B)
- Oddment of DK yarn in white (C)
- 1 pair each of 4mm (UK8:US6), 6mm (UK4:US10) and 8mm (UK0:US11) knitting needles
- Small amount of toy stuffing
- Blunt-ended tapestry needle
- 2 x dark brown 1 1/16 in (2.7cm) diameter buttons
- 2 x black 5/8 in (1.5cm) diameter buttons
- Sewing needle
- Black thread

sizes

To fit: child, up to 20in (51cm) head circumference [adult, up to 22in (56cm) head circumference]

tension

13 sts and 18 rows to 4in (10cm) over stocking stitch using 8mm needles and B. Use larger or smaller needles if necessary to obtain correct tension.

method

The hat is started with a 2 x 2 rib and then continued in stocking stitch. For the eyes, a picot edging is knitted first and white yarn is joined in to finish the eyeballs. The edging is folded towards the eyeball to form a rim, and the eyes are stuffed and stitched to the hat to peer through the fur. To finish, a large button is stitched to the centre of each eye for the iris, and smaller buttons are sewn on top for the pupils.

main section

With 6mm needles and A used doubled, cast on 60[64] sts.

child size only

Row 1 (RS): P1, (k2, p2) to last 3 sts, k2, p1.
Row 2 (WS): K1, (p2, k2) to last 3 sts, p2, k1.
Rows 3-4: As rows 1-2.

adult size only

Row 1 (RS): K1, (p2, k2) to last 3 sts, p2, k1.
Row 2 (WS): P1, (k2, p2) to last 3 sts, k2, p1.
Rows 3-4: As rows 1-2.

both sizes

Change to yarn B and 8mm needles.
Next row (RS) (inc): Kfb, k to end (61[65] sts).
Starting with a purl row, work in st st for 17[19] rows, ending with a WS row.

shape crown

Row 1 (RS) (dec): K2tog, (k12[13], sl1, k2tog, psso) 3 times, k12[13], k2togtbl (53[57] sts).
Row 2 (WS): Purl.
Row 3 (dec): K2tog, (k10[11], sl1, k2tog, psso) 3 times, k10[11], k2togtbl (45[49] sts).
Row 4: Purl.

Row 5 (dec): K2tog, (k8[9], sl1, k2tog, psso) 3 times, k8[9], k2togtbl (37[41] sts).
Row 6: Purl.
Row 7 (dec): K2tog, (k6[7], sl1, k2tog, psso) 3 times, k6[7], k2togtbl (29[33] sts).
Row 8: Purl.
Row 9 (dec): K2tog, (k4[5], sl1, k2tog, psso) 3 times, k4[5], k2togtbl (21[25] sts).
Row 10: Purl.
Row 11 (dec): K2tog, (k2[3], sl1, k2tog, psso) 3 times, k2[3], k2togtbl (13[17] sts).

adult size only

Row 12: Purl.
Row 13 (dec): K2tog, (k1, sl1, k2tog, psso) 3 times, k1, k2togtbl (9 sts).

both sizes

Break yarn and thread through rem sts, draw up tight and fasten off.

eyes (make 2)

With 4mm needles and A, cast on 30[32] sts.
Row 1 (RS): Knit.
Row 2 (WS): Purl.
Rows 3-4: Rep rows 1-2.

picot row

Row 5: K1, (yfd, k2tog) to last st, k1.
Row 6: Purl.
Rows 7-10: Rep rows 1-2 twice.

eyeball

Join and cont in C.
Rows 11-14: Rep rows 1-2 twice.
Row 15 (dec): (K2tog, k1[2]) 10[8] times (20[24] sts).
Row 16: Purl.
Row 17 (dec): (K2tog) 10[12] times (10[12] sts).
Row 18: Purl.
Break yarn, leaving a long length of each, and thread C through rem sts, draw up tight and fasten off.

making up

Join the back seam with mattress stitch (see page 124).

eyes

With the lengths of yarn left after fastening off, sew the side edges of the eye, matching the colours, to form a bowl shape. Turn under the lower edge at the picots and, on the wrong side of the work, slip stitch the cast-on edge to the stitches of the last row worked in A. Turn the picot edge towards the eyeball and sew the eye to the hat, just above the rib, stitching along the same edge as the slip stitches just worked and leaving an opening to stuff before closing. Place a small black button over the large brown button and sew to the centre of the eyeball. Weave in all the yarn ends.

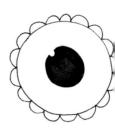

lining

See pages 130-138 for how to make and attach a cosy fleece or knitted lining.

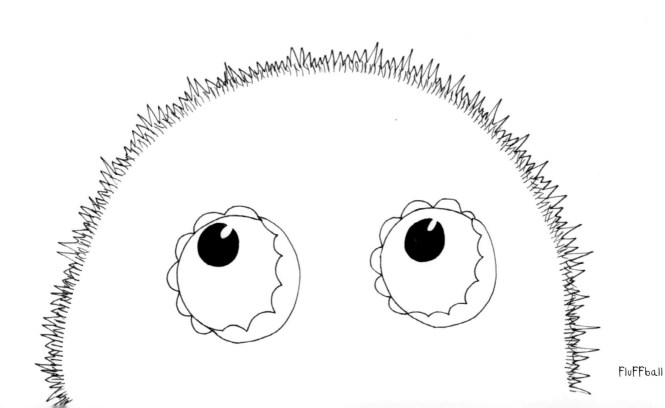

With sparkling eyes created using sequin-adorned yarn, this mutant fly hat with bendy antennae is sure to create a buzz whenever you wear it.

Fly

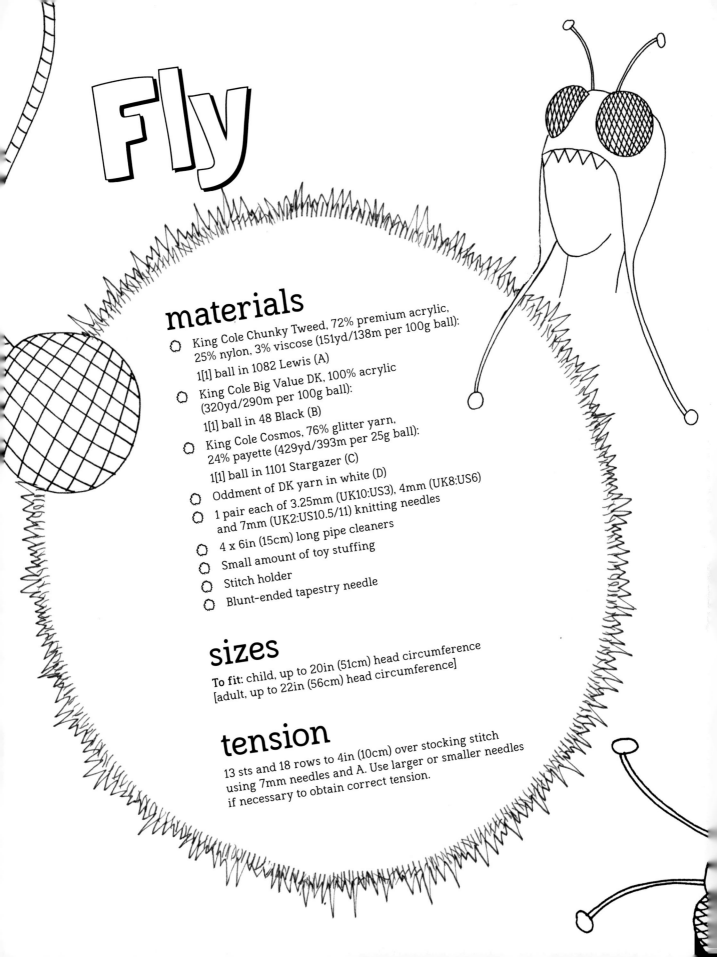

materials

- King Cole Chunky Tweed, 72% premium acrylic, 25% nylon, 3% viscose (151yd/138m per 100g ball):
  1[1] ball in 1082 Lewis (A)
- King Cole Big Value DK, 100% acrylic (320yd/290m per 100g ball):
  1[1] ball in 48 Black (B)
- King Cole Cosmos, 76% glitter yarn, 24% payette (429yd/393m per 25g ball):
  1[1] ball in 1101 Stargazer (C)
- Oddment of DK yarn in white (D)
- 1 pair each of 3.25mm (UK10:US3), 4mm (UK8:US6) and 7mm (UK2:US10.5/11) knitting needles
- 4 x 6in (15cm) long pipe cleaners
- Small amount of toy stuffing
- Stitch holder
- Blunt-ended tapestry needle

sizes

To fit: child, up to 20in (51cm) head circumference [adult, up to 22in (56cm) head circumference]

tension

13 sts and 18 rows to 4in (10cm) over stocking stitch using 7mm needles and A. Use larger or smaller needles if necessary to obtain correct tension.

method

The main part of the hat is knitted in one colour, starting with the earflaps and ending with the crown. The eyes are knitted in DK yarn together with a sequinned glitter fibre to catch the light, increasing the stitches to form a bowl shape when the side edges are joined. The eyes are stitched to the face and stuffed. Each antenna is made with a knitted strip that covers two pipe cleaners, twisted together to make it firmer. The antennae are topped with a knitted button-shaped tip, and the lower ends are stuffed to help them stand up on the hat. The teeth are knitted in one piece, from one side to the other, increasing and decreasing the stitches to form zigzags, then turned on its side and stitched across the lower edge of the face. Shimmery bobbles are knitted using the same yarns as the eyes and stitched to the ends of twisted cords that hang from the earflaps.

main section

Starting with the earflaps, with 7mm needles and A, follow the pattern for the main section of the Cyclops hat on page 63.

earflap facings

(make 2)

Omit if you plan to add a knitted lining.

With 7mm needles and A, follow the earflap facing pattern as for the Cyclops hat on page 64.

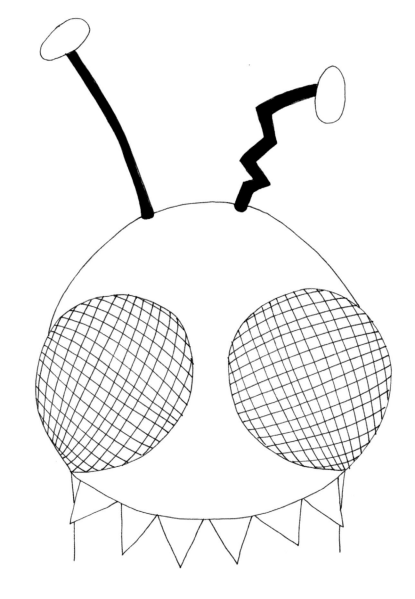

eyes *(make 2)*

With 4mm needles and yarns B and C held together, cast on 6 sts.
Row 1 (WS) (inc): (Kfb) 6 times (12 sts).
Row 2 (RS): Purl.
Row 3 (inc): (Kfb) 12 times (24 sts).
Row 4: Purl.
Row 5 (inc): (Kfb, k1) 12 times (36 sts).
Row 6: Purl.
Row 7 (inc): (Kfb, k2) 12 times (48 sts).
Row 8: Purl.

adult size only

Row 9 (inc): (Kfb, k3) 12 times (60 sts).
Row 10: Purl.

both sizes

Next: Starting with a k row, work 6 rows in st st, without shaping. Join and cont in A.
Next row: Purl.
Cast off k-wise, leaving a long length of A and B at the end.

antennae *(make 2)*

With 4mm needles and B, cast on 20[25] sts.
Starting with a k row, work 6 rows in st st.
Cast off, leaving a long length of yarn at the end.

antennae tip *(make 2)*

With 4mm needles and A, cast on 7 sts.
Starting with a p row, work 15 rows in rev st st, finishing on a RS row.
Cast off k-wise, leaving a long length of yarn at the end.

teeth

With 3.25mm needles and D, follow the pattern for the Yeti teeth on page 70.

knitted bobbles
(make 2)

With 4mm needles and yarns B and C held together, cast on 7 sts. Work as for the Cyclops eyeball pattern on page 64.

making up

Join the back seam with mattress stitch (see page 124). With RS together, sew the earflap facings, if applicable, to the earflaps, starting and finishing at the edge of the main section, leaving the overlapping cast-on edge open. Turn RS out and slip stitch the open edges to the inside of the main section.

eyes

Use the lengths of yarn left after fastening off to join the seam, forming a bowl shape. Sew each eye in place, just above the garter stitch edging at the lower end of the face, stitching neatly around the edges and leaving an opening to insert the stuffing before closing.

antennae

Twist two pipe cleaners together. Turn under the sharp edges and place the piece in the centre of the wrong side (purl side) of the knitted strip. Fold the strip around the pipe cleaners, bringing the long edges together. Use the length of yarn left after casting off to sew the edges together, encasing the pipe cleaners. Sew together the cast-on and cast-off edges of the tips of the antennae to form tubes. Gather the open edges at each end and work a few stitches through the centre to form a button shape. Stitch the knitted buttons to the top of the antennae. Use the end of a knitting needle to push a small amount of stuffing firmly into the first 3/4in (2cm) of the open end of each antenna. This will help them stand up when attached to the hat. Sew both antennae to the hat, setting them close together, halfway between the eyes and the top of the hat.

teeth

With the length of yarn left after casting off, stitch the row of teeth in place to the inside of the face, between the earflaps, sewing the top edge 5/8in (1.5cm) from the lower edge of the fly's face and stretching it slightly to fit.

finishing touches

If making a knitted lining, attach the twisted cords to the earflaps after joining the lining to the hat. Make two twisted cords (see page 126) using A, each measuring 8[12]in (20 [30]cm) long, using 6[8] strands of yarn. With the purl side of the work on the right side, sew the seam of each bobble, stuffing them before closing. Attach each to one end of the twisted cord, then stitch the other end of the cord to the tip of the earflap. Weave in all the yarn ends.

lining

See pages 130–138 for how to make and attach a cosy fleece or knitted lining.

Fiery

Flickering flames erupt from this volcanic hat, knitted in tweed and lava colours. The features are enhanced with a touch of shimmering yarn.

materials

- Lion Brand Heartland Tweed, 94% acrylic, 6% rayon (200yd/183m per 113g ball):
  1[1] ball in 350 Mount Ranier (A)
  1[1] ball in 113 Redwood (B)
  1[1] ball in 158 Yellowstone (C)
- Lion Brand Vanna's Glamour, 96% acrylic, 4% metallic polyester (202yd/185m per 50g ball):
  1[1] ball in 114 Red Stone (D)
- Oddment of DK yarn in white (E)
- 1 pair each of 3.25mm (UK10:US3), 4mm (UK8:US6) and 5mm (UK6:US8) knitting needles
- Small amount of toy stuffing
- Stitch holder
- Blunt-ended tapestry needle
- 2 x black $^3/_8$in (1cm) diameter buttons
- Sewing needle
- Black thread

sizes

To fit: child, up to 20in (51cm) head circumference [adult, up to 22in (56cm) head circumference]

tension

17 sts and 23 rows to 4in (10cm) over stocking stitch using 5mm needles and A. Use larger or smaller needles if necessary to obtain correct tension.

method

The main part of the hat starts with the earflaps and finishes at the shaping of the crown. The fiery wings and the teeth are worked from one side to the other and are shaped by increasing and decreasing stitches. The flames are knitted in three colours; they are shaped by slipping stitches and turning the work before the end of the row. The slipped stitches are eventually knitted together with the horizontal loop that lies before them, to prevent holes appearing in the work. The socket and the eye are knitted in one piece that is shaped by decreasing stitches and sewn together at the side edges. The eyebrows are shaped by increasing stitches, creating a curve in the work. The nostrils are embroidered in duplicate stitch, and the decoration on the fiery wings is worked in chain stitch. Tassels are attached to the ends of twisted cords that are stitched to the earflaps.

main section
first earflap

*With 5mm needles and A, cast on 3 sts.
Row 1 (inc) (RS): Kfb, k1, kfb (5 sts).
Row 2 (WS): K2, p1, k2.
Row 3 (inc): Kfb, k3, kfb (7 sts).
Row 4: K2, p3, k2.
Row 5 (inc): Kfb, k5, kfb (9 sts).
Row 6: K2, p5, k2.
Row 7 (inc): Kfb, k7, kfb (11 sts).
Row 8: K2, p7, k2.
Row 9 (inc): Kfb, k9, kfb (13 sts).
Row 10: K2, p9, k2.
Row 11 (inc): Kfb, k11, kfb (15 sts).
Row 12: K2, p11, k2.
Row 13 (inc): Kfb, k13, kfb (17 sts).
Row 14: K2, p13, k2.

Row 15 (inc): Kfb, k15, kfb (19 sts).
Row 16: K2, p15, k2.
Row 17 (inc): Kfb, k17, kfb (21 sts).
Row 18: K2, p17, k2.

adult size only
Row 19 (inc): Kfb, k19, kfb (23 sts).
Row 20: K2, p19, k2.

both sizes
Next row: Knit.
Next row: As row 18[20].*
Break yarn and leave these sts on a holder.

second earflap

Work as given for first earflap from * to *.
Next row: Cast on and knit 6 sts, knit across 21[23] sts of second earflap, turn and cast on 27 sts, turn and knit across 21[23] sts of first earflap, turn and cast on 6 sts (81[85] sts).
Next row (WS): K8, p17[19], k31, p17[19], k8.
Next row: Knit.
Rep last 2 rows once more.
Starting with a purl row, work 23[27] rows in st st.

shape crown

Row 1 (dec): K2tog, (k17[18], sl1, k2tog, psso) 3 times, k17[18], k2togtbl (73[77] sts).
Row 2: Purl.
Row 3 (dec): K2tog, (k15[16] sl1, k2tog, psso) 3 times, k15[16], k2togtbl (65[69] sts).
Row 4: Purl.
Row 5 (dec): K2tog, (k13[14], sl1, k2tog, psso) 3 times, k13[14], k2togtbl (57[61] sts).
Row 6: Purl.
Row 7 (dec): K2tog, (k11[12], sl1, k2tog, psso) 3 times, k11[12], k2togtbl (49[53] sts).

Row 8: Purl.
Row 9 (dec): K2tog, (k9[10], sl1, k2tog, psso) 3 times, k9[10], k2togtbl (41[45] sts).
Row 10: Purl.
Row 11 (dec): K2tog, (k7[8], sl1, k2tog, psso) 3 times, k7[8], k2togtbl (33[37] sts).
Row 12: Purl.
Row 13 (dec): K2tog, (k5[6], sl1, k2tog, psso) 3 times, k5[6], k2togtbl (25[29] sts).
Row 14: Purl.
Row 15 (dec): K2tog, (k3[4], sl1, k2tog, psso) 3 times, k3[4], k2togtbl (17[21] sts).
Break yarn and thread through rem sts, draw up tight and fasten off.

earflap facing
(make 2)

Omit if you plan to add a knitted lining.
With 5mm needles and A, cast on 3 sts and work the 20[22] rows as for the earflaps.
Next: Rep the last 2 rows 3 more times.
Cast off loosely.

fiery wings *(make 4)*

With 4mm needles and B, cast on 11 sts.
Row 1: K11.
Row 2 (inc): K10, kfb (12 sts).
Row 3 (inc): Kfb, k11 (13 sts).
Row 4 (inc): K12, kfb (14 sts).
Row 5 (inc): Kfb, k13 (15 sts).
Row 6 (inc): K14, kfb (16 sts).
Row 7 (inc): Kfb, k15 (17 sts).
Rows 8-11: K17.
Row 12 (dec): K15, k2tog (16 sts).
Row 13 (dec): K2tog, k14 (15 sts).
Row 14 (dec): K13, k2tog (14 sts).
Row 15 (dec): K2tog, k12 (13 sts).

Row 16 (inc): K12, kfb (14 sts).
Row 17 (inc): Kfb, k13 (15 sts).
Row 18 (inc): K14, kfb (16 sts).
Row 19 (inc): Kfb, k15 (17 sts).
Row 20 (inc): K16, kfb (18 sts).
Row 21 (inc): Kfb, k17 (19 sts).
Row 22 (dec): K2, k2tog, k15 (18 sts).
Rows 23-24: K18.
Row 25 (dec): K14, k2tog, k2 (17 sts).
Rows 26-27 (dec): Rep rows 12-13 (15 sts).
Rows 28 (dec): K2, k2tog, k9, k2tog (13 sts).
Row 29 (dec): K2tog, k11 (12 sts).
Row 30 (inc): K11, kfb (13 sts).
Row 31: Kfb, k8, k2tog, k2.
Row 32 (inc): K12, kfb (14 sts).
Row 33 (inc): Kfb, k13 (15 sts).
Row 34: K2, k2tog, k10, kfb.
Row 35 (inc): Kfb, k14 (16 sts).
Row 36 (inc): K15, kfb (17 sts).
Row 37 (dec): K13, k2tog, k2 (16 sts).
Rows 38-39: K16.
Row 40 (dec): K1, (k2tog) twice, k9, k2tog (13 sts).
Row 41 (dec): K2tog, k6, (k2tog) twice, k1 (10 sts).
Row 42 (dec): K1, (k2tog) twice, k3, k2tog (7 sts).
Row 43 (dec): (K2tog) 3 times, k1 (4 sts).
Cast off, leaving a long length of yarn at the end.

smaller wings *(make 2)*

Next: With 3.25mm needles and C, cast on 11 sts. Rep rows 1-43. Cast off, leaving a long length of yarn at the end.

flames *(make 7)*

With 3.25mm needles and B, cast on 16[18] sts.
Row 1: K15[17], turn.
Rows 2-3: Sl1, k13[15], turn.
Join and cont in D.
Row 4: Sl1, k11[13], turn.
Row 5: Sl1, k10[12], turn.
Row 6: Sl1, k9[11], turn.
Row 7: Sl1, k8[10], turn.
Join and cont in C.
Row 8: Sl1, k6[8], turn.
Row 9: Sl1, k5[7], turn.
Row 10: Sl1, k4[6], turn.
Row 11: Sl1, k4[6], pick up the horizontal loop before the next st and ktog with the next st to prevent a hole appearing in the work, turn.
Rows 12-15: Rep rows 10-11 twice.

Row 16: With D, sl1, k8[10], pick up the horizontal loop before the next st and ktog with the next st, turn.
Row 17: Sl1, k9[11], turn.
Row 18: Sl1, k10[12], pick up the horizontal loop before the next st and ktog with the next st, turn.
Row 19: Sl1, k11[13], pick up the horizontal loop before the next st and, with yarn B, ktog with the next st, turn.
Row 20: With B, sl1, k12[14], pick up the horizontal loop before the next st and ktog with the next st, k1, yfd, sl1.
Cast off.

eyes *(make 2)*
eye socket
With 3.25mm needles and A, cast on 15[20] sts.
Row 1 (RS): Purl.
Row 2 (WS): Knit.

eyeball
Join and cont in D.
Row 3: Knit.
Row 4: Purl.

adult size only
Row 5 (dec): (K2, k2tog) 5 times (15 sts).
Row 6: Purl.

both sizes
Next row (dec): (K1, k2tog) 5 times (10 sts).
Next row: Purl.
Break yarn and thread through rem sts, draw up to gather and fasten off, leaving a long length of A and D at the end.

eyebrows *(make 2)*
With 3.25mm needles and D, cast on 11[13] sts.
Row 1 (WS) (inc): (K1, kfb) 5[6] times, k1 (16[19] sts).
Row 2 (RS): Purl.
Cast off p-wise, leaving a long length of yarn at the end.

teeth
With 3.25mm needles and E, cast on 3 sts and follow the pattern for the Yeti teeth on page 70.

making up
Join the back seam with mattress stitch (see page 124). With RS together, sew the earflap facings, if applicable, to the earflaps, starting and finishing at the edge of the main section, leaving the overlapping cast-on edge open. Turn RS out and slip stitch the open edges to the inside of the main section.

fiery wings
With the length of yarn left after fastening off one piece, sew two larger pieces knitted in B together. Join the remaining two larger pieces in the same way. The remaining lengths of yarn will be used to stitch the wings to the hat. Place one smaller piece, worked in C, on top of one of the joined larger wings, matching the cast-on edges and the long curved edges. Use the length of yarn C, left after casting off, to stitch the lower curved edges together, starting from where the yarn is attached and ending at the lower corner of the wing. Flip the remaining pieces to reverse the shapes and place the smaller wing on top of the larger wing, matching the shaping, and stitching the lower edges together, as before. Embroider two lines in chain stitch on each wing, using yarn D, starting each line at the lower corner of the fiery wing and finishing between the peaks of the flames, stitching through all the layers. Sew a wing to each side of the hat using the remaining length of yarn left after casting off one of the pieces in B. Join the wing, knitted in B, to the side of the hat, stitching it from where the length of yarn is attached, down the long curved edge to the corner and along the

cast-on edge, leaving the shaping at the top unstitched.

flames
Sew the flames together at the base, joining them so they face in different directions. Stitch them securely to the top of the hat.

eyes
Use the lengths of A and D left after fastening off to sew the side edges of the eye together to form a cup shape, matching the yarns. Sew the eyes to the face, stitching carefully around the outside edges and leaving an opening to stuff them before closing. Sew a button to each eye.

eyebrows
Use the lengths of yarn left after casting off to sew the eyebrows to the hat above the eyes, with the cast-on stitches at the top so they curve upwards. Stitch all around the edges to attach them.

teeth and nostrils
With the length of yarn left after casting off, stitch the row of teeth in place to the inside of the hat between the earflaps, sewing the top edge of the teeth $5/8$in (1.5cm) from the lower edge of the hat and stretching the piece slightly to fit. Using yarn D doubled, embroider the nostrils in duplicate stitch (see page 129).

finishing touches
If making a knitted lining, attach the twisted cords to the earflaps after joining the lining to the hat. Make two twisted cords (see page 126) using A, each measuring 8[12]in (20[30]cm) long, using 8[10] strands of yarn. Make two tassels (see page 127) measuring 4[5$1/8$]in (10[13]cm)] long using yarns B and D together. Attach each to one end of the twisted cord, then stitch the other end of the cord to the tip of the earflap. Weave in all the yarn ends.

lining
See pages 130–138 for how to make and attach a cosy fleece or knitted lining.

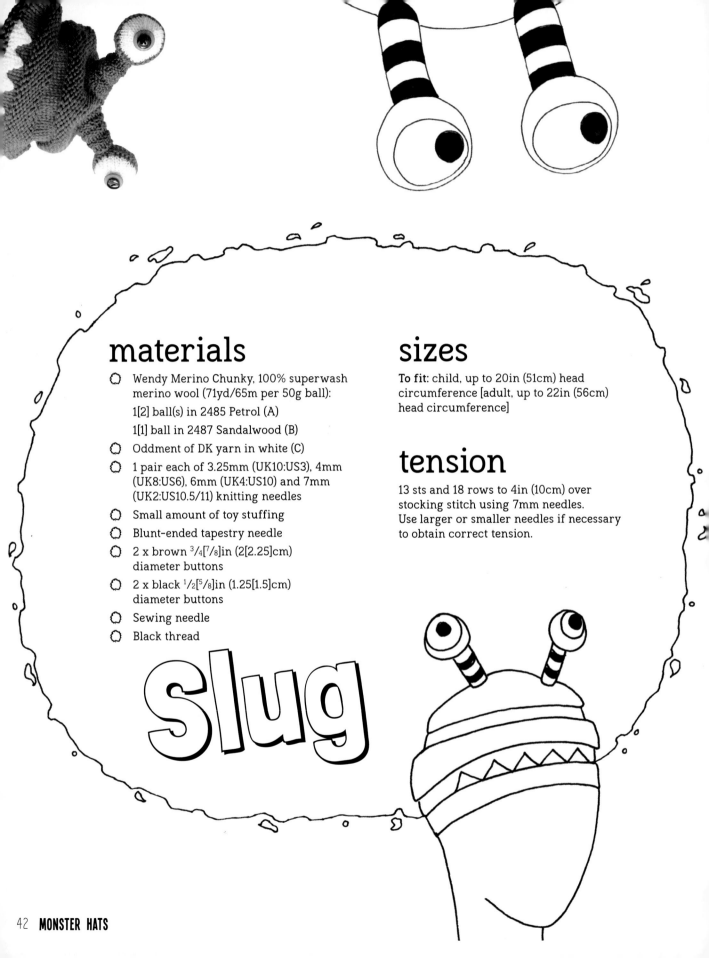

materials

- Wendy Merino Chunky, 100% superwash merino wool (71yd/65m per 50g ball):
  1[2] ball(s) in 2485 Petrol (A)
  1[1] ball in 2487 Sandalwood (B)
- Oddment of DK yarn in white (C)
- 1 pair each of 3.25mm (UK10:US3), 4mm (UK8:US6), 6mm (UK4:US10) and 7mm (UK2:US10.5/11) knitting needles
- Small amount of toy stuffing
- Blunt-ended tapestry needle
- 2 x brown $^{3}/_{4}[^{7}/_{8}]$in (2[2.25]cm) diameter buttons
- 2 x black $^{1}/_{2}[^{5}/_{8}]$in (1.25[1.5]cm) diameter buttons
- Sewing needle
- Black thread

sizes

To fit: child, up to 20in (51cm) head circumference [adult, up to 22in (56cm) head circumference]

tension

13 sts and 18 rows to 4in (10cm) over stocking stitch using 7mm needles. Use larger or smaller needles if necessary to obtain correct tension.

Slug

Knitted in stocking stitch and reverse stocking stitch to add a rippled texture to the brightly coloured stripes, this slug hat oozes fun.

method

The hat is started with a band of garter stitch to prevent the lower edge from curling up. The stripes are formed with bands of a contrasting colour worked in stocking stitch, with the main colour knitted in reverse stocking stitch. The row of teeth is knitted from side to side, increasing and decreasing the stitches to produce zigzags. These are stitched to the front of the hat. The eyeballs and sockets are knitted in one piece, increasing the stitches from the back of the eye, then decreasing the stitches to shape the eyeball at the front. The eyes are attached to knitted stalks, alternating the yarns to form the stripes. Buttons are sewn on to finish the features.

main section

With 6mm needles and A, cast on 61[65] sts.
Work 5 rows in garter st.
Change to 7mm needles.
Join and cont in B.
Row 1 (RS): Knit.
Row 2 (WS): Purl.
Rows 3-6: Rep rows 1-2 twice.
Row 7: With A, knit.
Rows 8-13: With A, rep rows 1-6.
Row 14: With A, knit.
Rows 15-20: With B, rep rows 1-6.
Row 21: With A, knit.
With A, starting with a k row, work 7[9] rows in rev st st, ending with a WS row.

shape crown

Cont in A as follows:
Row 1 (WS) (dec): P2tog, (p12[13], sl1, p2tog, psso) 3 times, p12[13], p2tog (53[57] sts).
Row 2 (RS): Knit.

Row 3 (dec): P2tog, (p10[11], sl1, p2tog, psso) 3 times, p10[11], p2tog (45[49] sts).
Row 4: Knit.
Row 5 (dec): P2tog, (p8[9], sl1, p2tog, psso) 3 times, p8[9], p2tog (37[41] sts).
Row 6: Knit.
Row 7 (dec): P2tog, (p6[7], sl1, p2tog, psso) 3 times, p6[7], p2tog (29[33] sts).
Row 8: Knit.
Row 9 (dec): P2tog, (p4[5], sl1, p2tog, psso) 3 times, p4[5], p2tog (21[25] sts).
Row 10: Knit.
Row 11 (dec): P2tog, (p2[3], sl1, p2tog, psso) 3 times, p2[3], p2tog (13[17] sts).

adult size only

Row 12: Knit.
Row 13 (dec): P2tog, (p1, sl1, p2tog, psso) 3 times, p1, p2tog (9 sts).

both sizes

Break yarn and thread through rem sts, draw up tight and fasten off.

eyes (make 2)
eye stalk

With 4mm needles and B, cast on 24 sts.
Row 1 (WS): Knit.
Row 2 (RS) (dec): K1, (k2tog, k2) 5 times, k2tog, k1 (18 sts).
Join in A.
Rows 3-4: With A, purl.
Row 5: With A, knit.
Row 6 (dec): (K1, k2tog) 6 times (12 sts).
Rows 7-8: With B, purl.
Rows 9-10: With B, knit.
Rows 11-12: With A, purl.
Rows 13-14: With A, knit.
Rows 15-16: With B, purl.

Cast off k-wise, leaving a long length of B at the end.

eye socket

With 4mm needles and B, cast on 7 sts.
Row 1 (WS) (inc): (Kfb) 6 times, k1 (13 sts).
Row 2 (RS): Purl.
Row 3 (inc): (K1, kfb) 6 times, k1 (19 sts).
Row 4: Purl.
Row 5 (inc): (K2, kfb) 6 times, k1 (25 sts).

adult size only

Row 6: Purl.
Row 7 (inc): (K3, kfb) 6 times, k1 (31 sts).

both sizes

Next: Purl 3 rows.
Next row: Knit.

eyeball

Join and cont in C.
Row 1 (RS): Knit.
Row 2 (WS): Purl.

adult size only

Row 3 (dec): (K3, k2tog) 6 times, k1 (25 sts).
Row 4: Purl.

both sizes

Next row (dec): (K2, k2tog) 6 times, k1 (19 sts).
Next row: Purl.
Next row (dec): (K1, k2tog) 6 times, k1 (13 sts).
Break yarn and thread through rem sts, draw up to gather and fasten off, leaving a long length of B and C at the end.

teeth

With 3.25mm needles and C, cast on 2 sts.
Row 1 (inc): K1, kfb (3 sts).
Row 2 (inc): Kfb, k2 (4 sts).
Row 3 (inc): K3, kfb (5 sts).
Row 4 (inc): Kfb, k4 (6 sts).
Row 5 (inc): K5, kfb (7 sts).

adult size only

Row 6 (inc): Kfb, k6 (8 sts).
Row 7 (dec): K6, k2tog (7 sts).

both sizes

Next row (dec): K2tog, k5 (6 sts).
Next row (dec): K4, k2tog (5 sts).
Next row (dec): K2tog, k3 (4 sts).
Next row (dec): K2, k2tog (3 sts).
Next row (dec): K2tog, k1 (2 sts).
This makes one tooth. Repeat to complete six teeth.
Cast off, leaving a long length of yarn at the end.

making up

Join the back seam with mattress stitch (see page 124).

eyes

Use the length of yarn left after fastening off to join the seam of the stalk. Sew the sides of the eyeball and socket together, and stuff before closing the seam. Sew each eye to the narrow top end of a stalk, so it stands on its side. Stuff the stalks firmly. Stitch the wide, lower edges of each stalk next to each other, positioning them just below the top of the hat, with the eyes facing forwards. Place a black button over a larger brown button and sew to the centre of each eye.

teeth

Position the teeth in the centre of the front of the hat, on the first section of stocking stitch worked in B. Stitch neatly around the edges. Weave in all the yarn ends.

lining

See pages 130–138 for how to make and attach a cosy fleece or knitted lining.

materials

- Cascade Pacific Chunky, 60% acrylic, 40% merino wool (120yd/110m per 100g ball):
  1[1] ball in 16 Spring Green (A)
  1[1] ball in 53 Beet (B)
  1[1] ball in 44 Italian Plum (C)
- Oddment of DK yarn in white (D)
- 1 pair each of 3.25mm (UK10:US3), 4mm (UK8:US6) and 6.5mm (UK3:US10.5) knitting needles
- Small amount of toy stuffing
- Stitch holder
- Blunt-ended tapestry needle
- 2 x dark brown $1^{1}/_{16}$in (2.7cm) diameter buttons
- 2 x black $^{5}/_{8}$in (1.5cm) diameter buttons
- Sewing needle
- Black thread

sizes

To fit: child, up to 20in (51cm) head circumference [adult, up to 22in (56cm) head circumference]

tension

13 sts and 18 rows to 4in (10cm) over stocking stitch using 6.5mm needles. Use larger or smaller needles if necessary to obtain correct tension.

Fang

This monstrous reptile hat features large, glaring eyes, protruding fangs and a row of spikes running down the back of its head.

Row 10 (inc): K11, kfb (13 sts).
Row 11 (dec): K2tog, k11 (12 sts).
Row 12 (dec): K10, k2tog (11 sts).
Row 13 (dec): K2tog, k9 (10 sts).
Row 14 (dec): K8, k2tog (9 sts).
Row 15 (dec): K2tog, k7 (8 sts).
Row 16 (dec): K6, k2tog (7 sts).
Row 17 (dec): K2tog, k5 (6 sts).
Row 18 (dec): K4, k2tog (5 sts).
Row 19 dec): K2tog, k3 (4 sts).
Repeat rows 2-19 11 times more (12 points).
Cast off, leaving a long length of yarn at the end.

method

The main part of the hat is knitted first, beginning with the earflaps. The spikes running over the top of the head are knitted from side to side and shaped by increasing and decreasing stitches to form points. Double the number of points are knitted so the piece can be folded in half and sewn together to form a line of cone shapes that are stuffed and stitched to the hat. The socket and eye are each knitted in one piece, shaped by decreasing stitches and then sewn together at the side edges to form cup shapes. The eyes are stuffed, stitched to the hat and finished with buttons. The fangs are shaped by decreasing the central stitches. The side edges are sewn together and the fangs are stuffed and stitched to the lower edge of the front of the hat. Tassels are sewn to striped twisted cords that are attached to the earflaps.

main section

Starting with the earflaps, with 6.5mm needles and A, follow the pattern for the main section of the Cyclops hat on page 63.

earflap facings
(make 2)

Omit if you plan to add a knitted lining.
With 6.5mm needles and A, follow the earflap facing pattern as for the Cyclops hat on page 64.

spikes

With 4mm needles and B, cast on 4 sts.
Row 1: K4.
Row 2 (inc): K3, kfb (5 sts).
Row 3 (inc): Kfb, k4 (6 sts).
Row 4 (inc): K5, kfb (7 sts).
Row 5 (inc): Kfb, k6 (8 sts).
Row 6 (inc): K7, kfb (9 sts).
Row 7 (inc): Kfb, k8 (10 sts).
Row 8 (inc): K9, kfb (11 sts).
Row 9 (inc): Kfb, k10 (12 sts).

eyes *(make 2)*
eye socket

With 4mm needles and C, cast on 20[25] sts.
Row 1 (RS): Purl.
Row 2 (WS): Knit.
Row 3: Purl.

eyeball

Join and cont in D.
Rows 4-6: As rows 1-3.

adult size only

Row 9 (dec): (K3, k2tog) 5 times (20 sts).
Row 8: Purl.

both sizes

Next row (dec): (K2, k2tog) 5 times (15 sts).
Next row: Purl.
Next row (dec): (K1, k2tog) 5 times (10 sts).
Next row: Purl.
Break yarn and thread through rem sts, draw up to gather and fasten off, leaving a long length of C and D at the end.

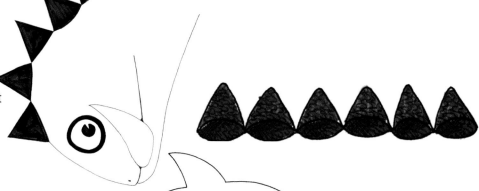

fangs *(make 2)*

With 3.25mm needles and D, cast on 15[17] sts.
Row 1 (RS): Knit.
Row 2 (WS): Purl.

adult size only

Row 3 (RS) (dec): K7, sl1, k2tog, psso, k7 (15 sts).
Row 4: Purl.
Row 5: Knit.
Row 6: Purl.

both sizes

Next row (dec): K6, sl1, k2tog, psso, k6 (13 sts).
Work 3 rows in st st.
Next row (dec): K5, sl1, k2tog, psso, k5 (11 sts).
Work 3 rows in st st.
Next row (dec): K4, sl1, k2tog, psso, k4 (9 sts).
Work 3 rows in st st.
Next row (dec): K3, sl1, k2tog, psso, k3 (7 sts).
Work 3 rows in st st.
Next row (dec): K2, sl1, k2tog, psso, k2 (5 sts).
Next row: Purl.
Break yarn and thread through rem sts. Fasten off, leaving a long length of yarn at the end.

making up

Join the back seam with mattress stitch (see page 124). With RS together, sew the earflap facings, if applicable, to the earflaps, starting and finishing at the edge of the main section, leaving the overlapping cast-on edge open. Turn RS out and slip stitch the open edges to the inside of the main section.

> When making up the spikes, stitch the lower edges together between each spike.

spikes

Fold the knitted spikes in half lengthways, matching the shaping. Sew together the narrow end and the pointed edges and stitch the lower edges together between each spike. Stuff the spikes and sew the piece to the centre of the hat, covering the back seam and over the crown shaping at the front.

eyes

Use the lengths of C and D left after fastening off to sew the side edges of the eye together to form a cup shape, matching the colours. Sew the eyes to the face, just above the reverse stocking stitch edging, stitching carefully around the outside edges and leaving an opening to stuff them before closing. Place a small black button over the large brown button and sew to the centre of each eyeball. Weave in all the yarn ends.

fangs

Sew the side edges of the fang together and stuff lightly, keeping the shape flat. With the seam positioned at the centre back, stitch the lower edges of the fang together. Place a fang on either side of the eyes. Stitch the lower edges of the hat and fangs together. Work a few hidden stitches halfway up the back of the fangs and into the hat to hold them in place.

finishing touches

If making a knitted lining, attach the twisted cords to the earflaps after joining the lining to the hat. Make two striped cords (see page 126) using A and B, each measuring 8[12]in (20[30]cm) long, using 3[4] strands of yarn of each colour (6[8] strands in total for each cord). Make two tassels (see page 127) measuring 4[5⅛]in (10[13]cm)] long in C, and attach each to one end of the twisted cord, then stitch the other end of the cord to the tip of the earflap. Weave in all the yarn ends.

lining

See pages 130–138 for how to make and attach a cosy fleece or knitted lining.

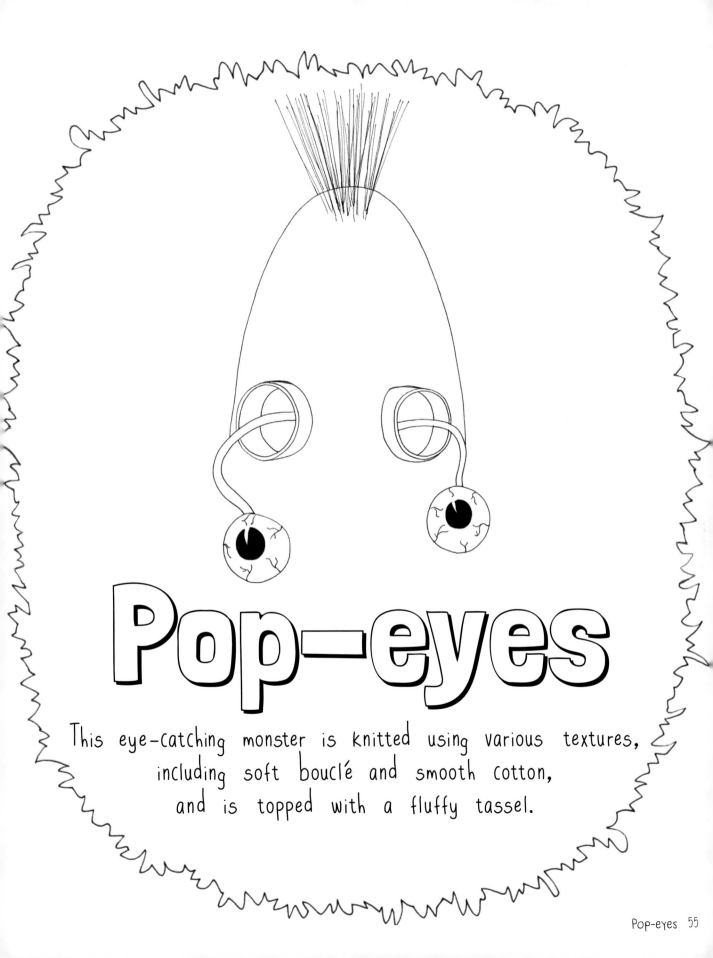

Pop-eyes

This eye-catching monster is knitted using various textures,
including soft bouclé and smooth cotton,
and is topped with a fluffy tassel.

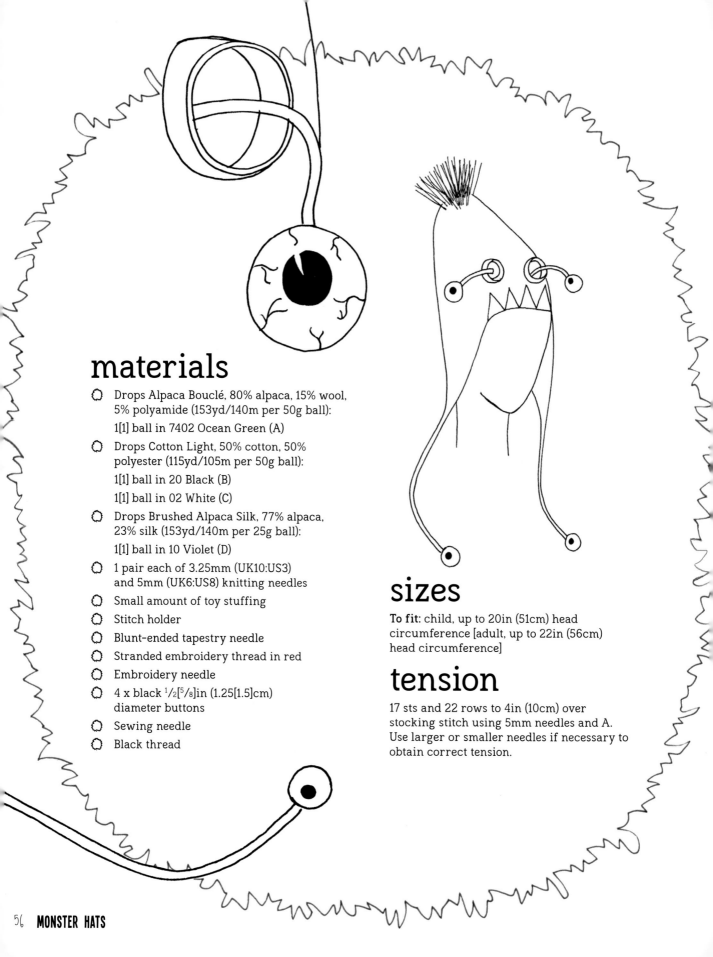

materials

- Drops Alpaca Bouclé, 80% alpaca, 15% wool, 5% polyamide (153yd/140m per 50g ball):
  1[1] ball in 7402 Ocean Green (A)
- Drops Cotton Light, 50% cotton, 50% polyester (115yd/105m per 50g ball):
  1[1] ball in 20 Black (B)
  1[1] ball in 02 White (C)
- Drops Brushed Alpaca Silk, 77% alpaca, 23% silk (153yd/140m per 25g ball):
  1[1] ball in 10 Violet (D)
- 1 pair each of 3.25mm (UK10:US3) and 5mm (UK6:US8) knitting needles
- Small amount of toy stuffing
- Stitch holder
- Blunt-ended tapestry needle
- Stranded embroidery thread in red
- Embroidery needle
- 4 x black $\frac{1}{2}[\frac{5}{8}]$in (1.25[1.5]cm) diameter buttons
- Sewing needle
- Black thread

sizes

To fit: child, up to 20in (51cm) head circumference [adult, up to 22in (56cm) head circumference]

tension

17 sts and 22 rows to 4in (10cm) over stocking stitch using 5mm needles and A. Use larger or smaller needles if necessary to obtain correct tension.

method

The main part of the hat is knitted first, starting with the earflaps. The top of the hat is lengthened by working three rows straight after each row of decreasing. The eyes that pop out of their sockets are knitted in one piece, decreasing and increasing rows to shape them. The side edges are sewn together and decorated with embroidered veins and button pupils. The large eyes that hang from the twisted cords are also knitted in one piece and finished in the same way. The teeth are knitted in garter stitch and worked from one side to the other. They are shaped by increasing and decreasing stitches to form points. The piece is turned on its side and stitched to the front of the hat. The tufty hair is a tassel that is attached to the top of the hat.

main section
first earflap

*With 5mm needles and A, cast on 3 sts.
Row 1 (inc) (RS): Kfb, k1, kfb (5 sts).
Row 2 (WS): K2, p1, k2.
Row 3 (inc): Kfb, k3, kfb (7 sts).
Row 4: K2, p3, k2.
Row 5 (inc): Kfb, k5, kfb (9 sts).
Row 6: K2, p5, k2.
Row 7 (inc): Kfb, k7, kfb (11 sts).
Row 8: K2, p7, k2.
Row 9 (inc): Kfb, k9, kfb (13 sts).
Row 10: K2, p9, k2.
Row 11 (inc): Kfb, k11, kfb (15 sts).
Row 12: K2, p11, k2.
Row 13 (inc): Kfb, k13, kfb (17 sts).
Row 14: K2, p13, k2.
Row 15 (inc): Kfb, k15, kfb (19 sts).
Row 16: K2, p15, k2.
Row 17 (inc): Kfb, k17, kfb (21 sts).
Row 18: K2, p17, k2.

adult size only

Row 19 (inc): Kfb, k19, kfb (23 sts).
Row 20: K2, p19, k2.

both sizes

Next row: Knit.
Next row: As row 18[20].*
Break yarn and leave these sts on a holder.

second earflap

Work as given for first earflap from * to *.
Next row: Cast on and knit 6 sts, knit across 21[23] sts of second earflap, turn and cast on 27 sts, turn and knit across 21[23] sts of first earflap, turn and cast on 6 sts (81[85] sts).
Next row (WS): K8, p17[19], k31, p17[19], k8.
Next row: Knit.
Rep last 2 rows once more.
Starting with a purl row, work 23[27] rows in st st.

shape crown

Row 1 (dec): K2tog, (k17[18], sl1, k2tog, psso) 3 times, k17[18], k2togtbl (73[77] sts).
Row 2: Purl.
Row 3: Knit.
Row 4: Purl.
Row 5 (dec): K2tog, (k15[16], sl1, k2tog, psso) 3 times, k15[16], k2togtbl (65[69] sts).
Row 6: Purl.
Row 7: Knit.
Row 8: Purl.
Row 9 (dec): K2tog, (k13[14], sl1, k2tog, psso) 3 times, k13[14], k2togtbl (57[61] sts).
Row 10: Purl.
Row 11: Knit.
Row 12: Purl.
Row 13 (dec): K2tog, (k11[12], sl1, k2tog, psso) 3 times, k11[12], k2togtbl (49[53] sts).

Row 14: Purl.
Row 15: Knit.
Row 16: Purl.
Row 17 (dec): K2tog, (k9[10], sl1, k2tog, psso) 3 times, k9[10], k2togtbl (41[45] sts).
Row 18: Purl.
Row 19: Knit.
Row 20: Purl.
Row 21 (dec): K2tog, (k7[8], sl1, k2tog, psso) 3 times, k7[8], k2togtbl (33[37] sts).
Row 22: Purl.
Row 23: Knit.
Row 24: Purl.
Row 25 (dec): K2tog, (k5[6], sl1, k2tog, psso) 3 times, k5[6], k2togtbl (25[29] sts).
Row 26: Purl.
Row 27: Knit.
Row 28: Purl.
Row 29 (dec): K2tog, (k3[4], sl1, k2tog, psso) 3 times, k3[4], k2togtbl (17[21] sts).
Break yarn and thread through rem sts, draw up tight and fasten off.

earflap facing
(make 2)
Omit if you plan to add a knitted lining.
With 5mm needles and A, cast on 3 sts and work the 20[22] rows as for the earflaps.
Next: Rep the last 2 rows 3 more times.
Cast off loosely.

eyes on stalks

(make 2)

eye sockets

With 3.25mm needles and A, cast on 30 sts.
Row 1 (RS): Purl.
Row 2 (WS): Knit.
Join and cont in B.
Row 3: Knit.
Row 4: Purl.
Row 5 (dec): (K3, k2tog) 6 times (24 sts).
Row 6: Purl.
Row 7 (dec): (K2, k2tog) 6 times (18 sts).
Row 8: Purl.
Row 9 (dec): (K1, k2tog) 6 times (12 sts).
Row 10 (dec): (P2tog) 6 times (6 sts).

stalk

Join and cont in C.
Row 11: Knit.
Row 12: Purl.
Rows 13–14: As rows 11–12.
Row 15 (dec): (K1, k2tog) twice (4 sts).
Starting with a p row, work in st st, until the stalk measures 2in (5cm) ending on a WS row.

eyeball

Row 1 (RS) (inc): (Kfb) 4 times (8 sts).
Row 2 (WS): Purl.
Row 3 (inc): (K1, kfb) 4 times (12 sts).
Row 4: Purl.
Row 5 (inc): (K1, kfb) 6 times (18 sts).
Row 6: Purl.
Row 7 (inc): (K2, kfb) 6 times (24 sts).
Row 8: Purl.
Row 9: Knit.
Row 10: Purl.
Row 11 (dec): (K2, k2tog) 6 times (18 sts).

Row 12: Purl.
Row 13 (dec): (K1, k2tog) 6 times (12 sts).
Break yarn and thread through rem sts, draw up tight and fasten off, leaving a long length of each yarn at the end.

large eyeballs

(make 2)

socket

With 5mm needles and A, cast on 7 sts.
Row 1 (WS) (inc): (Kfb) 6 times, k1 (13 sts).
Row 2 (RS): Purl.
Row 3 (inc): (K1, kfb) 6 times, k1 (19 sts).
Row 4: Purl.
Row 5 (inc): (K2, kfb) 6 times, k1 (25 sts).
Row 6: Purl.
Row 7 (inc): (K3, kfb) 6 times, k1 (31 sts).
Next: Purl 3 rows.
Next row: Knit.

eyeball

Change to 3.25mm needles.
Join and cont in C.
Row 1 (RS): Knit.
Row 2 (WS): Purl.
Rows 3–4: As rows 1–2.
Row 5 (dec): (K3, k2tog) 6 times, k1 (25 sts).
Row 6: Purl.
Row 7 (dec): (K2, k2tog) 6 times, k1 (19 sts).
Row 8: Purl.
Row 9 (dec): (K1, k2tog) 6 times, k1 (13 sts).
Break yarn and thread through rem sts, draw up to gather and fasten off, leaving a long length of A and C at the end.

teeth

With 3.25mm needles and C, cast on 2 sts.
Row 1: K2.
Row 2 (inc): K1, kfb (3 sts).
Row 3 (inc): Kfb, k2 (4 sts).
Row 4 (inc): K3, kfb (5 sts).
Row 5 (inc): Kfb, k4 (6 sts).
Row 6 (inc): K5, kfb (7 sts).
Row 7 (inc): Kfb, k6 (8 sts).
Row 8 (inc): K7, kfb (9 sts).
Row 9 (dec): K2tog, k7 (8 sts).
Row 10 (dec): K6, k2tog (7 sts).
Row 11 (dec): K2tog, k5 (6 sts).
Row 12 (dec): K4, k2tog (5 sts).
Row 13 (dec): K2tog, k3 (4 sts).
Row 14 (dec): K2, k2tog (3 sts).
Row 15 (dec): K2tog, k1 (2 sts).
Repeat rows 2–15 3 times more (4 teeth).
Cast off, leaving a long length of yarn at the end.

making up

Join the back seam with mattress stitch (see page 124). With RS together, sew the earflap facings, if applicable, to the earflaps, starting and finishing at the edge of the main section, leaving the overlapping cast-on edge open. Turn RS out and slip stitch the open edges to the inside of the main section.

eyes on stalks

With the length of yarn left at the end, sew the side edges of the eyeball together, leaving an opening to stuff it. Stitch the opening in the eyeball to close and then sew the edges of the stalk and eye socket together, matching the yarns. Use the end of a knitting needle to push some stuffing firmly into the base of the stalk.

This will help it stand out from the eyeball socket. Using three strands of embroidery thread, embroider the veins of the eye in chain stitch (see page 129). Sew a button to the centre of each eyeball. Turn up the two rows knitted in A to form a lip. Sew the eye sockets to the hat, stitching around the edges of the piece worked in B so the first two rows stand out. Work a few stitches through the base of the stalk and into the hat to keep the socket flat.

large eyeballs

With the lengths of yarn left after fastening off, sew together the side edges of the eyeball and socket, leaving an opening to stuff the eye firmly before closing. Using three strands of embroidery thread, embroider veins on the eye in chain stitch. Sew a button to the centre of each eye.

teeth

Position the teeth in the centre of the front of the hat, just above the garter stitch edging. Stitch neatly around the edges.

tassel

Make a tassel (see page 127) measuring $2^3/4[3^1/8]$in (7[8]cm) long in D, and sew securely to the top of the hat.

finishing touches

If making a knitted lining, attach the twisted cords to the earflaps after joining the lining to the hat. Make two twisted cords (see page 126) using A, each measuring 8[12]in (20[30]cm) long, using 10[12] strands of yarn. Sew the large eyeballs to one end of each twisted cord. Stitch the other end of the cord to the tip of the earflap, so the eyeballs face forwards. Weave in all the yarn ends.

lining

See pages 130–138 for how to make and attach a cosy fleece or knitted lining.

One large staring eye
glares out from under
a massive horn on this
striking hat. With claws
that hang from the
ends of twisted cords
too, this hat certainly
demands attention.

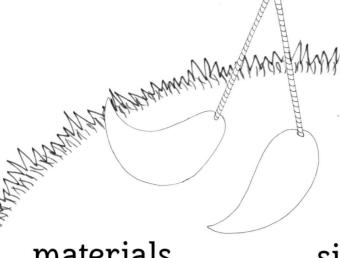

materials

- Hayfield Baby Chunky, 70% acrylic, 30% nylon (170yd/155m per 100g ball):
  1[1] ball in 405 Applebob (A)
  1[1] ball in 400 White (B)
  1[1] ball in 415 Tangy Tangerine (C)
- Oddment of chunky yarn in black (D)
- 1 pair each of 6mm (UK4:US10) and 7mm (UK2:US10.5/11) knitting needles
- Small amount of toy stuffing
- Stitch holder
- Blunt-ended tapestry needle
- 1 x black $1/2[5/8]$in (1.25[1.5]cm) diameter button
- Sewing needle
- Black thread

sizes

To fit: child, up to 20in (51cm) head circumference [adult, up to 22in (56cm) head circumference]

tension

13 sts and 18 rows to 4in (10cm) over stocking stitch using 7mm needles. Use larger or smaller needles if necessary to obtain correct tension.

Cyclops

method

The basic hat shape is knitted first, starting with the earflaps. The eyeball is knitted in rows and shaped by increasing and then decreasing stitches. Then the seam is stitched together and the eyeball is stuffed. The pupil is knitted in rows and the edges are joined to form a disc. The eye is finished with embroidered details to the pupil and a small button. The eyeball is stitched into a knitted socket with an eyelid formed by working short rows. The horn and claws are shaped in the same way as the crown of the hat, decreasing two stitches at a time up the centre of the pieces. They are stuffed and attached to the hat, with the addition of twisted cords to finish.

main section
first earflap
*With 7mm needles and A, cast on 3 sts.
Row 1 (inc) (RS): Kfb, k1, kfb (5 sts).
Row 2 (WS): K2, p1, k2.
Row 3 (inc): Kfb, k3, kfb (7 sts).
Row 4: K2, p3, k2.
Row 5 (inc): Kfb, k5, kfb (9 sts).
Row 6: K2, p5, k2.
Row 7 (inc): Kfb, k7, kfb (11 sts).
Row 8: K2, p7, k2.
Row 9 (inc): Kfb, k9, kfb (13 sts).
Row 10: K2, p9, k2.
Row 11 (inc): Kfb, k11, kfb (15 sts).
Row 12: K2, p11, k2.

adult size only
Row 13 (inc): Kfb, k13, kfb (17 sts).
Row 14: K2, p13, k2.

both sizes
Next row: Knit.
Next row: As row 12[14].*
Break yarn and leave these sts on a holder.

second earflap
Work as given for first earflap from * to *.
Next row: Cast on and knit 5 sts, knit across 15[17] sts of second earflap, turn and cast on 21 sts, turn and knit across 15[17] sts of first earflap, turn and cast on 5 sts (61[65] sts).
Next row (WS): K7, p11[13], k25, p11[13], k7.
Next row: Knit.
Rep last 2 rows once more and then, starting with a p row, work 19[21] rows in st st, ending with a WS row.

shape crown
Row 1 (RS) (dec): K2tog, (k12[13], sl1, k2tog, psso) 3 times, k12[13], k2togtbl (53[57] sts).
Row 2 (WS): Purl.
Row 3 (dec): K2tog, (k10[11], sl1, k2tog, psso) 3 times, k10[11], k2togtbl (45[49] sts).
Row 4: Purl.
Row 5 (dec): K2tog, (k8[9], sl1, k2tog, psso) 3 times, k8[9], k2togtbl (37[41] sts).

Row 6: Purl.
Row 7 (dec): K2tog, (k6[7], sl1, k2tog, psso) 3 times, k6[7], k2togtbl (29[33] sts).
Row 8: Purl.
Row 9 (dec): K2tog, (k4[5], sl1, k2tog, psso) 3 times, k4[5], k2togtbl (21[25] sts).
Row 10: Purl.
Row 11 (dec): K2tog, (k2[3], sl1, k2tog, psso) 3 times, k2[3], k2togtbl (13[17] sts).

adult size only
Row 12: Purl.
Row 13 (dec): K2tog, (k1, sl1, k2tog, psso) 3 times, k1, k2togtbl (9 sts).

both sizes
Break yarn and thread through rem sts, draw up tight and fasten off.

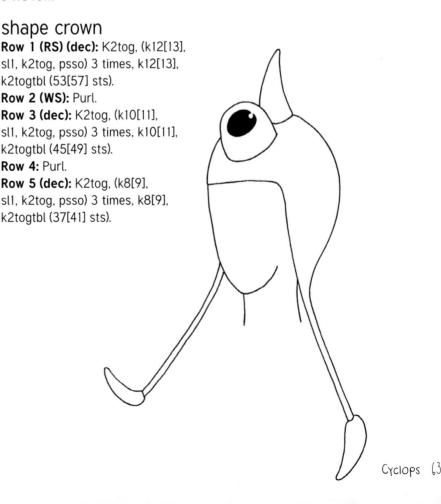

Cyclops 63

earflap facing
(make 2)

Omit if you plan to add a knitted lining.

With 7mm needles and A, cast on 3 sts and work the 14[16] rows as for the earflaps.

Next: Rep the last 2 rows 3 more times.

Cast off loosely.

pupil

With 6mm needles and D, cast on 25 sts.

Join and cont in C.

Row 1 (RS) (dec): (K2, k2tog) 6 times, k1 (19 sts).

Row 2 (WS): Purl.

Row 3 (dec): (K1, k2tog) 6 times, k1 (13 sts).

Break yarn and thread through rem sts, draw up to gather and fasten off.

eyeball

With 6mm needles and B, cast on 7 sts.

Row 1 (RS) (inc): (Kfb) 6 times, k1 (13 sts).

Row 2 (WS): Purl.

Row 3 (inc): (K1, kfb) 6 times, k1 (19 sts).

Row 4: Purl.

Row 5 (inc): (K2, kfb) 6 times, k1 (25 sts).

Row 6: Purl.

adult size only

Row 7 (inc): (K3, kfb) 6 times, k1 (31 sts).

Row 8: Purl.

both sizes

Starting with a k row, work 2 rows in st st.

adult size only

Next row (dec): (K3, k2tog) 6 times, k1 (25 sts).

Next row: Purl.

both sizes

Next row (dec): (K2, k2tog) 6 times, k1 (19 sts).

Next row: Purl.

Next row (dec): (K1, k2tog) 6 times, k1 (13 sts).

Next row: Purl.

Next row (dec): (K2tog) 6 times, k1 (7 sts).

Break yarn and thread through rem sts, draw up to gather and fasten off.

eye socket

With 6mm needles and A, cast on 7 sts.

Rows 1–6[1–8]: Work rows 1–6[1–8] as given for the eyeball (25[31] sts).

shape eyelid

Row 1 (RS): P20[25], turn.

Row 2 (WS): Sl1 p-wise, k14[18], turn.

Row 3: Sl1 p-wise, p13[17], turn.

Row 4: Sl1 p-wise, k12[16], turn.

adult size only

Row 5: Sl1 p-wise, p15, turn.

Row 6: Sl1 p-wise, k14, turn.

both sizes

Next row: Sl1 p-wise, p12[14], (pick up the horizontal loop before the next st and ptog with the next st to prevent a hole appearing in the work) 2[3] times, p to end.

Next row: K19[23], (pick up the horizontal loop before the next st and ktog with the next st) 2[3] times, k to end.

Next row: Purl.

Cast off k-wise.

horn

With 7mm needles and C doubled, cast on (13[17] sts).

Starting with a k row, work 4 rows st st.

adult size only

Next row (RS) (dec): K7, sl1 p-wise, k2tog, psso, k7 (15 sts).

Work 3 rows st st.

**Next row (dec): K6, sl1 p-wise, k2tog, psso, k6 (13 sts).

Work 3 rows st st.

both sizes

Next row (dec): K5, sl1 p-wise, k2tog, psso, k5 (11 sts).

Work 3 rows st st.

*Next row (dec): K4, sl1 p-wise, k2tog, psso, k4 (9 sts).

Next row: Purl.

Next row (dec): K3, sl1 p-wise, k2tog, psso, k3 (7 sts).

Next row: Purl.

Next row (dec): K2, sl1 p-wise, k2tog, psso, k2 (5 sts).

Next row: Purl.

Next row (dec): K1, sl1 p-wise, k2tog, psso, k1 (3 sts).

Break yarn and thread through rem sts. Fasten off.

claws *(make 2)*

With 7mm needles and C doubled, cast on 6[8] sts.

Row 1 (inc): (Kfb) 5[7] times, k1 (11[15] sts).

Starting with a p row, work 3 rows st st.

Work from *[**] as given for the horn.

making up

Join the back seam with mattress stitch (see page 124). With RS together, sew the earflap facings, if applicable, to the earflaps, starting and finishing at the edge of the main section, leaving the overlapping cast-on edge open. Turn RS out and slip stitch the open edges to the inside of the main section.

horn

Join the seam of the horn. Stuff firmly and sew to the top of the hat, matching the back seam of the horn with the gathered top of the crown, so the horn curves towards the back. Stitch all around the lower edges of the horn to attach it securely.

eye

Sew the seam of the eyeball, stuffing the piece before closing and fastening off securely. Sew the pupil neatly to the centre front of the eyeball. With D, embroider straight lines of irregular lengths, from the cast-on edge towards the centre of the pupil. Join the back seam of the eye socket. Slip the eyeball inside and stitch carefully in place. The eyelid will overlap the top edge of the pupil. Sew the button to the centre of the pupil and embroider the reflection of light in the eye by working one or two sets of short, straight stitches in B. Attach the eye to the centre front of the hat with the eyelid at the top, sewing through each stitch of the first row of the eyelid shaping, so it sits flat against the hat.

finishing touches

If making a knitted lining, attach the twisted cords to the earflaps after joining the lining to the hat. Make two twisted cords (see page 126) using A, each measuring 8[12]in (20[30]cm) long, using 6[8] strands of yarn. Sew the seam of each claw, stuffing them before closing. Attach each to one end of the twisted cord, then stitch the other end of the cord to the tip of the earflap. Weave in all the yarn ends.

lining

See pages 130–138 for how to make and attach a cosy fleece or knitted lining.

The yeti has an icy cold stare, but its soft fur, knitted in a fleecy yarn, gives this monster hat a warm and cuddly feel.

materials

- Robin Fleece Chunky, 100% nylon (104yd/95m per 100g ball):
  1[1] ball in 4221 White (A)
- Robin Chunky, 100% acrylic (153yd/140m per 100g ball):
  1[1] ball in 0132 Storm (B)
- Oddment of DK yarn in white (C)
- 1 pair each of 3.25mm (UK10:US3), 4mm (UK8:US6) and 6.5mm (UK3:US10.5) knitting needles
- Stitch holder
- Blunt-ended tapestry needle
- 2 x pale blue $^3/_4$[$^7/_8$]in (2[2.25]cm) diameter buttons
- 2 x black $^1/_2$[$^5/_8$]in (1.25[1.5]cm) diameter buttons
- Sewing needle
- Black thread

sizes

To fit: child, up to 20in (51cm) head circumference [adult, up to 22in (56cm) head circumference]

tension

13 sts and 18 rows to 4in (10cm) over stocking stitch using A and 6.5mm needles. Use larger or smaller needles if necessary to obtain correct tension.

yeti

method

The earflaps are knitted first and then worked into the main part of the hat. The face is worked in intarsia in a contrasting yarn. The eyes are knitted in rows, on smaller needles, starting with the chunky yarn that was used for the face and then continuing with DK yarn for the whites of the eyes. The stitches are decreased and the seams joined to form a disc. The teeth are knitted in rows, increasing and decreasing the stitches to form zigzags. The piece is turned on its side and stitched across the lower edge of the face. To finish the features, buttons are sewn to the centre of each eye and the nostrils are embroidered onto the face. Knitted snowballs hang from twisted cords that are attached to the earflaps.

main section

Before starting, wind around 40g (1½oz) of yarn A into a separate ball, ready to use for the shaping of the Yeti's face.

first earflap

*With 6.5mm needles and A, cast on 3 sts.
Row 1 (inc) (RS): Kfb, k1, kfb (5 sts).
Row 2 (WS): K2, p1, k2.
Row 3 (inc): Kfb, k3, kfb (7 sts).
Row 4: K2, p3, k2.
Row 5 (inc): Kfb, k5, kfb (9 sts).
Row 6: K2, p5, k2.
Row 7 (inc): Kfb, k7, kfb (11 sts).
Row 8: K2, p7, k2.
Row 9 (inc): Kfb, k9, kfb (13 sts).
Row 10: K2, p9, k2.
Row 11 (inc): Kfb, k11, kfb (15 sts).
Row 12: K2, p11, k2.

adult size only

Row 13 (inc): Kfb, k13, kfb (17 sts).
Row 14: K2, p13, k2.

both sizes

Next row: Knit.
Next row: As row 12[14].*
Break yarn and leave these sts on a holder.

second earflap

Work as given for first earflap from * to *.

face

The following is worked in intarsia (see page 123):
Next: Using A, cast on and k 5 sts, knit across 15[17] sts of second earflap, turn.
Join in B and cast on 21 sts, turn. Join in the second ball of A, knit across 15[17] sts of first earflap, turn and cast on 5 sts in A (61[65] sts).
Next row (WS): K7A, p11[13]A, k2A, k21B, k2A, p11[13]A, k7A.
Next row: K20[22]A, k21B, k20[22]A.
Rep the last 2 rows once more.
Next row (WS): P20[22]A, p21B, p20[22]A.
Next row (RS): K20[22]A, k21B, k20[22]A.
Rep last 2 rows 4[5] times more, then rep the first of the last 2 rows once again to end with a WS row.

shape top of face

Work next 8 rows in patt from the chart on page 71 or as given below:
Row 1: K21[23]A, k19B, k21[23]A.
Row 2: P22[24]A, p17B, p22[24]A.
Row 3: K23[25]A, k15B, k23[25]A.
Row 4: P24[26]A, p13B, p24[26]A.
Row 5: K25[27]A, k11B, k25[27]A.
Row 6: P26[28]A, p9B, p26[28]A.
Cont in A.
Row 7: Knit.
Row 8: Purl.

shape crown

Row 1 (RS) (dec): K2tog, (k12[13], sl1, k2tog, psso) 3 times, k12[13], k2togtbl (53[57] sts).
Row 2 (WS): Purl.
Row 3 (dec): K2tog, (k10[11], sl1, k2tog, psso) 3 times, k10[11], k2togtbl (45[49] sts).
Row 4: Purl.
Row 5 (dec): K2tog, (k8[9], sl1, k2tog, psso) 3 times, k8[9], k2togtbl (37[41] sts).
Row 6: Purl.
Row 7 (dec): K2tog, (k6[7], sl1, k2tog, psso) 3 times, k6[7], k2togtbl (29[33] sts).
Row 8: Purl.
Row 9 (dec): K2tog, (k4[5], sl1, k2tog, psso) 3 times, k4[5], k2togtbl (21[25] sts).
Row 10: Purl.
Row 11 (dec): K2tog, (k2[3], sl1, k2tog, psso) 3 times, k2[3], k2togtbl (13[17] sts).

adult size only

Row 12: Purl.
Row 13 (dec): K2tog, (k1, sl1, k2tog, psso) 3 times, k1, k2togtbl (9 sts).

both sizes

Break yarn and thread through rem sts, draw up tight and fasten off.

earflap facing
(make 2)

Omit if you plan to add a knitted lining.

With 6.5mm needles and A, cast on 3 sts and work the 14[16] rows as for the earflaps.

Next: Rep the last 2 rows 3 more times.

Cast off loosely.

eyes *(make 2)*

With 4mm needles and B, cast on 30[32] sts.

Row 1 (RS): Purl.

Join and cont in C.

Row 2 (WS): Purl.

Row 3 (dec): (K2tog, k1[2]) 10[8] times (20[24] sts).

Row 4: Purl.

Row 5 (dec): (K2tog) 10[12] times (10[12] sts).

Row 6: Purl.

Row 7 (dec): (K2tog) 5[6] times (5[6] sts).

Break yarn and thread through rem sts, draw up tight and fasten off, leaving a long length of both colours at the end.

teeth

With 3.25mm needles and C, cast on 3 sts.

Row 1: K3.

Row 2 (inc): K2, kfb (4 sts).

Row 3 (inc): Kfb, k3 (5 sts).

Row 4 (inc): K4, kfb (6 sts).

Row 5 (inc): Kfb, k5 (7 sts).

Row 6 (inc): K6, kfb (8 sts).

Row 7 (dec): K2tog, k6 (7 sts).

Row 8 (dec): K5, k2tog (6 sts).

Row 9 (dec): K2tog, k4 (5 sts).

Row 10 (dec): K3, k2tog (4 sts).

Row 11 (dec): K2tog, k2 (3 sts).

Rows 2–11 make one tooth. Rep until the row of teeth reaches across the lower edge of the face when slightly stretched.

Cast off, leaving a long length of yarn at the end.

snowballs *(make 2)*

With 6.5mm needles and A, cast on 7 sts.

Work as for the Cyclops eyeball pattern on page 64.

making up

Join the back seam with mattress stitch (see page 124). With RS together, sew the earflap facings, if applicable, to the earflaps, starting and finishing at the edge of the main section, leaving the overlapping cast-on edge open. Turn RS out and slip stitch the open edges to the inside of the main section.

eyes

Thread the yarn left after fastening off the eye onto a blunt-ended needle. Sew the side edges together to form a disc, matching the colours. Sew the eyes to the face, stitching carefully around the outside edges. Place a black button over a larger blue button and sew to the centre of each eye.

teeth

With the length of yarn left after casting off, stitch the row of teeth in place to the inside of the face, between the earflaps, sewing the top edge 5/8in (1.5cm) from the lower edge of the face and stretching it slightly to fit. The garter stitch edge of the face will form the top lip of the monster.

nose

With yarn C, embroider the nostrils in satin stitch (see page 129).

finishing touches

If making a knitted lining, attach the twisted cords to the earflaps after joining the lining to the hat. Make two twisted cords (see page 126) using B, each measuring 8[12]in (20[30]cm) long, using 6[8] strands of yarn. Sew the seam of each snowball, stuffing them before closing and fastening off securely. Attach each to one end of the twisted cord, then stitch the other end of the cord to the tip of the earflap. Weave in all the yarn ends.

lining

See pages 130–138 for how to make and attach a cosy fleece or knitted lining.

yeti chart

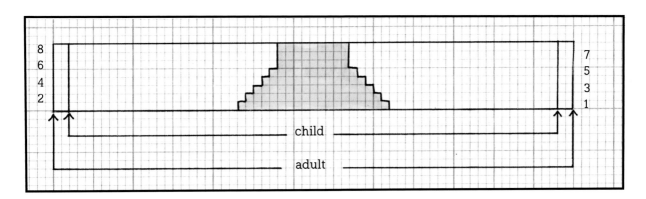

8
6
4
2

7
5
3
1

child

adult

Key

☐ k on RS, p on WS

☐ yarn A

▨ yarn B

Zombie

Featuring scary scars and unseeing eyes, this zombie hat is what the fashionable undead are wearing this season. It's topped off with a hair-raising mane of curls.

materials

- Debbie Bliss Rialto Chunky, 100% wool (65yd/60m per 50g ball):
  1[2] ball in 43001 Black (A)
  2[2] balls in 43032 Iris (B)
- Oddment of chunky yarn in white (C)
- Oddment of DK yarn in black (D)
- 1 pair each of 4mm (UK8:US6), 6mm (UK4:US10) and 7mm (UK2:US10.5/11) knitting needles
- Small amount of toy stuffing
- Blunt-ended tapestry needle
- 2 x black ⅝in (1.5cm) diameter buttons
- Sewing needle
- Black thread

sizes

To fit: child, up to 20in (51cm) head circumference [adult, up to 22in (56cm) head circumference]

tension

13 sts and 18 rows to 4in (10cm) over stocking stitch using 7mm needles. Use larger or smaller needles if necessary to obtain correct tension.

special abbreviation

ML: Make loop
See page 122 for illustrated instructions.

method

The hat begins with a rib and then a few rows of reverse stocking stitch to form the top lip. The crown of the hat is shaped on the wrong side of the work and loops are knitted into the right-side rows to produce the zombie's hair. The socket and eye are knitted in one piece that is shaped by decreasing stitches and sewn together at the side edges. The eyes are stuffed so they pop out when stitched to the hat. The nostrils and the teeth are worked in duplicate stitch and the scars are embroidered in chain stitch.

main section

With 6mm needles and A, cast on 59[63] sts.
Row 1 (RS): K2[1], p1, (k2, p1) to last 2[1] st(s), k2[1].
Row 2 (WS): P2[1], k1, (p2, k1) to last 2[1] st(s), p2[1].
Rows 3-4: As rows 1-2.
Join and cont in B.
Change to 7mm needles.
Row 5 (RS) (inc): Kfb, k to last st, kfb (61[65] sts).
Cont in rev st st as follows:
Row 6 (WS): Knit.
Row 7: Purl.
Row 8: Knit.

Starting with a knit row, work in st st for 14[16] rows, ending with a WS row. Rejoin and cont in A.
Next row (RS): Knit.
Next row (WS): Knit.
Next row: Purl.

shape crown
Row 1 (WS) (dec): P2tog, (p12[13], sl1, p2tog, psso) 3 times, p12[13], p2tog (53[57] sts).
Row 2 (RS): K1, (ML) to last st, k1.
Row 3 (dec): P2tog, (p10[11], sl1, p2tog, psso) 3 times, p10[11], p2tog (45[49] sts).

Row 4: As row 2.
Row 5 (dec): P2tog, (p8[9], sl1, p2tog, psso) 3 times, p8[9], p2tog (37[41] sts).
Row 6: As row 2.
Row 7 (dec): P2tog, (p6[7], sl1, p2tog, psso) 3 times, p6[7], p2tog (29[33] sts).
Row 8: As row 2.
Row 9 (dec): P2tog, (p4[5], sl1, p2tog, psso) 3 times, p4[5], p2tog (21[25] sts).
Row 10: As row 2.
Row 11 (dec): P2tog, (p2[3], sl1, p2tog, psso) 3 times, p2[3], p2tog (13[17] sts).
Row 12: As row 2.

adult size only
Row 13: As row 2.
Row 14 (dec): P2tog, (p1, sl1, p2tog, psso) 3 times, p1, p2tog (9 sts).

both sizes
Break yarn and thread through rem sts, draw up tight and fasten off.

eyes *(make 2)*
eye socket
With 4mm needles and B, cast on 18[24] sts.
Row 1 (RS): Purl.
Row 2 (WS): Knit.

eyeball
Join and cont in C.
Row 3: Knit.
Row 4: Purl.

adult size only
Row 5 (dec): (K2, k2tog) 6 times (18 sts).
Row 6: Purl.

both sizes
Next row (dec): (K1, k2tog) 6 times (12 sts).
Next row: Purl.
Break yarn and thread through rem sts, draw up to gather and fasten off, leaving a long length of B and C at the end.

making up
Join the back seam with mattress stitch, matching the colours (see page 124).

eyes
Use the lengths of B and C left after fastening off to sew the side edges of the eye together to form a cup shape, matching the colours. Sew the eyes to the face, just above the reverse stocking stitch edging, stitching carefully around the outside edges and leaving an opening to stuff them before closing. Sew a button to each eye.

teeth, nostrils and scars
Use the duplicate stitch (see page 129) and yarn C to embroider six teeth on the central knit stitches of the ribbing, working over two columns of four rows of rib and the two cast-on stitches at the lower edge to form each tooth. Using yarn A, embroider the nostrils in duplicate stitch. Embroider the scars using D, working in chain stitch (see page 129). Weave in all the yarn ends.

lining
See pages 130–138 for how to make and attach a cosy fleece or knitted lining.

Alien

This monster is out of this world, featuring a cable design down the centre of the head, and embroidered details to enhance the glistening gaze of the bug-eyed alien.

materials

- Wendy Serenity Chunky, 70% acrylic, 20% alpaca, 10% wool (87yd/80m per 100g ball): 1[1] ball in 3205 Oyster (A)
- Wendy Supreme Luxury Cotton DK, 100% cotton (219yd/201m per 100g ball): 1[1] ball in 1949 Poppy Red (B)
- Twilleys of Stamford Goldfingering, 80% viscose, 20% metalized polyester (109yd/100m per 25g ball): 1[1] ball in 38 Red (C)
- Oddment of DK yarn in black (D)
- 1 pair each of 4mm (UK8:US6), 6mm (UK4:US10) and 7mm (UK2:US10.5/11) knitting needles
- Cable needle
- Small amount of toy stuffing
- 2 x 6in (15cm) long pipe cleaners
- Blunt-ended tapestry needle

sizes

To fit: child, up to 20in (51cm) head circumference [adult, up to 22in (56cm) head circumference]

tension

13 sts and 18 rows to 4in (10cm) over stocking stitch using 7mm needles and A. Use larger or smaller needles if necessary to obtain correct tension.

special abbreviations

C4B: Sl 2 sts onto cable needle and hold at back of work, k2, k2 from cable needle

C4F: Sl 2 sts onto cable needle and hold at front of work, k2, k2 from cable needle

method

The hat is started with a wide rib. A cable design is worked in the centre of the main piece, knitted in stocking stitch. The shaping of the eyes is begun by slipping the first stitch and turning the work before the last stitch of each row, working one less stitch each time. The shaping is finished by knitting into one extra stitch at the end of each row, until all the stitches are back on the same needle. These are stuffed, stitched to the hat and finished with embroidery in duplicate stitch. The antennae are made from knitted strips covering pipe cleaners. These are topped with a knitted button. The lower ends of the antennae are stuffed to help them stand up on the hat. The nostrils are two duplicate stitches embroidered onto the rib of the hat.

main section

With 6mm needles and A, cast on 59[63] sts.

child size only
Row 1 (RS): K1, (p2, k3) to last 3 sts, p2, k1.
Row 2 (WS): P1, (k2, p3) to last 3 sts, k2, p1.
Rows 3-4: As rows 1-2.

adult size only
Row 1 (RS): (K3, p2) to last 3 sts, k3.
Row 2 (WS): (P3, k2) to last 3 sts, p3.
Rows 3-4: As rows 1-2.

Made using yarns that produce
a blend of hot hues and a touch
of shimmer, this demon hat
has a fiery, glowing effect.

Demon

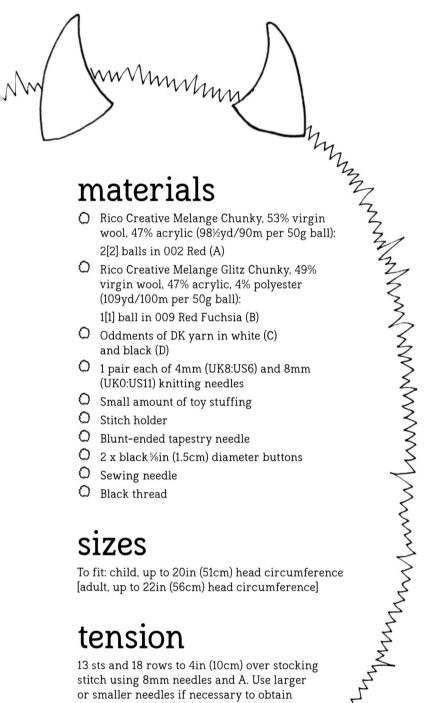

materials

- ○ Rico Creative Melange Chunky, 53% virgin wool, 47% acrylic (98½yd/90m per 50g ball): 2[2] balls in 002 Red (A)
- ○ Rico Creative Melange Glitz Chunky, 49% virgin wool, 47% acrylic, 4% polyester (109yd/100m per 50g ball): 1[1] ball in 009 Red Fuchsia (B)
- ○ Oddments of DK yarn in white (C) and black (D)
- ○ 1 pair each of 4mm (UK8:US6) and 8mm (UK0:US11) knitting needles
- ○ Small amount of toy stuffing
- ○ Stitch holder
- ○ Blunt-ended tapestry needle
- ○ 2 x black ⅝in (1.5cm) diameter buttons
- ○ Sewing needle
- ○ Black thread

sizes

To fit: child, up to 20in (51cm) head circumference [adult, up to 22in (56cm) head circumference]

tension

13 sts and 18 rows to 4in (10cm) over stocking stitch using 8mm needles and A. Use larger or smaller needles if necessary to obtain correct tension.

method

The main piece of the hat is knitted first, starting at the earflaps and finishing with the shaping of the crown. The eyes are shaped by slipping stitches at each end. They are sewn in place at an angle to the front of the hat, then buttons are stitched to the centre of each eye. The large and small horns are shaped by decreasing the central stitches. The side edges are joined and the horns are stuffed firmly before being stitched in place on the hat. Large tassels hang from twisted cords that are stitched to the ends of the earflaps to finish the hat.

main section

Starting with the earflaps, with 8mm needles and A, follow the pattern for the main section of the Cyclops hat on page 63.

earflap facings
(make 2)

Omit if you plan to add a knitted lining. With 8mm needles and A, follow the earflap facing pattern as for the Cyclops hat on page 64.

eyes *(make 2)*

With 4mm needles and A, cast on 12[14] sts.
Row 1 (RS): Purl.
Join and cont in C.
Row 2 (WS): Sl1, p to last st, sl1.
Row 3: Sl2, k to last 2 sts, sl2.
Row 4: Sl3, p to last 3 sts, sl3.
Row 5: Sl3, k to last 3 sts, sl3.
Row 6: Sl2, p to last 2 sts, sl2.
Row 7: Sl1, k to last st, sl1.
Rows 8-9: With A, p to end.
Cast off k-wise, leaving a long length of yarn A at the end.

large horns *(make 2)*

With 4mm needles and B, cast on
17[21] sts.
Rows 1-6: Starting with a k row,
work 6 rows in st st.
Row 7 (RS) (dec): K7[9], sl1, k2tog,
psso, k7[9] (15[19] sts).
Row 8: Purl.
Row 9: Knit.
Row 10: Purl.
Row 11 (dec): K6[8], sl1, k2tog, psso,
k6[8] (13[17] sts).
Row 12: Purl.
Row 13: Knit.
Row 14: Purl.
Row 15 (dec): K5[7], sl1, k2tog,
psso, k5[7] (11[15] sts).
Row 16: Purl.
Row 17: Knit.
Row 18: Purl.
Row 19 (dec): K4[6], sl1, k2tog, psso,
k4[6] (9[13] sts).
Row 20: Purl.
Row 21: Knit.
Row 22: Purl.
Row 23 (dec): K3[5], sl1, k2tog,
psso, k3[5] (7[11] sts).
Row 24: Purl.
Row 25: Knit.
Row 26: Purl.
Row 27 (dec): K2[4], sl1, k2tog,
psso, k2[4] (5[9] sts).

adult size only

Row 28: Purl.
Row 29: Knit.
Row 30: Purl.
Row 31 (dec): K3, sl1, k2tog, psso,
k3 (7 sts).
Row 32: Purl.
Row 33: Knit.
Row 34: Purl.
Row 35 (dec): K2, sl1, k2tog, psso,
k2 (5 sts).

both sizes

Break yarn and thread through rem
sts. Fasten off, leaving a long length
of yarn at the end.

small horns *(make 2)*

With 4mm needles and D, cast
on 13[15] sts.
Row 1: Knit.
Row 2: Purl.
Work rows 15-23[19-31] as given for
the large horns.
Break yarn and thread through rem
sts. Fasten off, leaving a long length
of yarn at the end.

making up

Join the back seam with mattress
stitch (see page 124). With RS
together, sew the earflap facings,
if applicable, to the earflaps, starting
and finishing at the edge of the
main section, leaving the overlapping
cast-on edge open. Turn RS out and
slip stitch the open edges to the
inside of the main section.

eyes

Sew the eyes to the hat, positioning
them at an angle, with the cast-on
edge at the top of the eye. Stitch
a button to the centre of the whites
of each eye.

horns

Sew the side edges of the horns
together. Stuff the horns firmly.
Sew a large horn to each side of the
hat, just below the top, stitching all
around the lower edges to attach
them securely. Sew the small horns
close to each other, above the eyes.

finishing touches

If making a knitted lining, attach the
twisted cords to the earflaps after
joining the lining to the hat. Make two
twisted cords (see page 126) using A,
each measuring 8[12]in (20[30]cm)
long, using 6[8] strands of yarn. Make
two tassels (see page 127) measuring
4[5$\frac{1}{8}$]in (10[13]cm) long in B. Attach
each to one end of the twisted cord,
then stitch the other end of the cord
to the tip of the earflap. Weave in all
the yarn ends.

lining

See pages 130-138 for how to
make and attach a cosy fleece
or knitted lining.

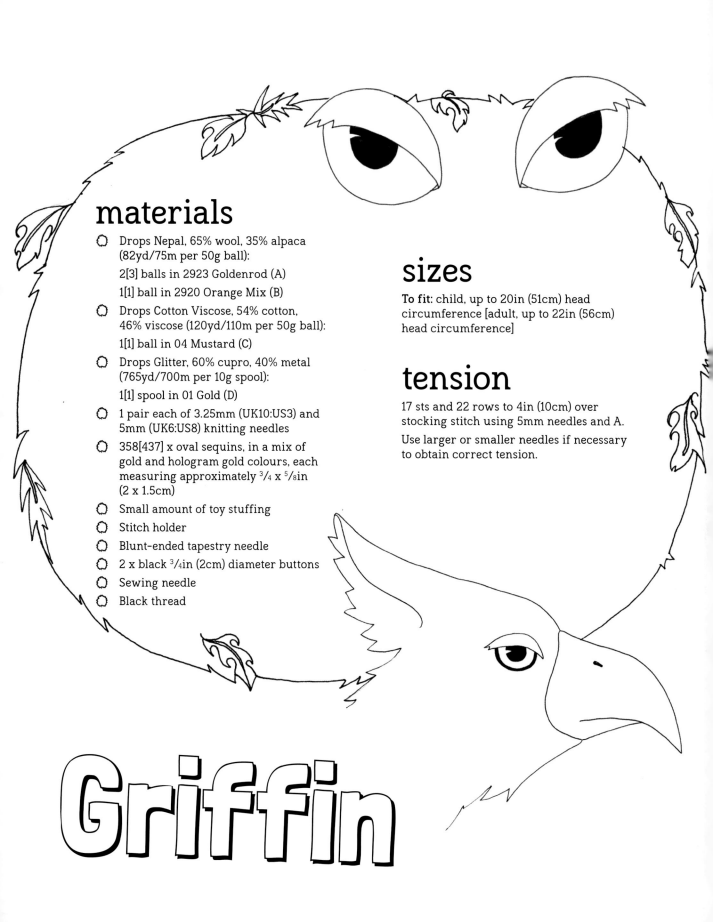

materials

- Drops Nepal, 65% wool, 35% alpaca (82yd/75m per 50g ball):

  2[3] balls in 2923 Goldenrod (A)

  1[1] ball in 2920 Orange Mix (B)

- Drops Cotton Viscose, 54% cotton, 46% viscose (120yd/110m per 50g ball):

  1[1] ball in 04 Mustard (C)

- Drops Glitter, 60% cupro, 40% metal (765yd/700m per 10g spool):

  1[1] spool in 01 Gold (D)

- 1 pair each of 3.25mm (UK10:US3) and 5mm (UK6:US8) knitting needles

- 358[437] x oval sequins, in a mix of gold and hologram gold colours, each measuring approximately $^{3}/_{4}$ x $^{5}/_{8}$in (2 x 1.5cm)

- Small amount of toy stuffing
- Stitch holder
- Blunt-ended tapestry needle
- 2 x black $^{3}/_{4}$in (2cm) diameter buttons
- Sewing needle
- Black thread

sizes

To fit: child, up to 20in (51cm) head circumference [adult, up to 22in (56cm) head circumference]

tension

17 sts and 22 rows to 4in (10cm) over stocking stitch using 5mm needles and A.

Use larger or smaller needles if necessary to obtain correct tension.

Griffin

This curious creature,
which is half lion,
half eagle, is made
with metallic thread
running through its
beak and hundreds
of sequins knitted
into the fabric.

method

The earflaps are knitted first, starting at the pointed ends. Each sequin is attached by sliding it against the work and purling the next stitch, so it lays at the front of the work. Charts are included to show the placement of the sequins. The eyes are shaped, starting at the top of the eyelid, by slipping the first stitch and turning before the last stitch, working one less stitch at each end of the row and then knitting into one extra stitch at each end, finishing at the lower lid. The beak is shaped by decreasing the centre stitches on every row, finishing at the narrow tip.

The ears are each made in two pieces, forming the inner ear and the sequinned outer ear. Buttons finish the eyes and tassels hang from the ends of twisted cords, attached to the earflaps.

main section

Before commencing, thread the sequins on to the yarn. Thread a needle with sewing thread, doubled to form a loop at the end. Thread the yarn through the loop. Insert the needle through the hole in the sequin, pushing the sequin right along the length of the thread and onto the yarn (see below).

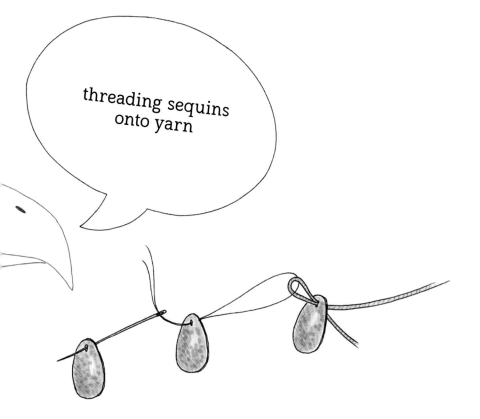

threading sequins onto yarn

first earflap

Following the charts on pages 94–95, and with 5mm needles and A, cast on 3 sts.
Row 1 (inc) (RS): Kfb, k1, kfb (5 sts).
Row 2 (WS): K2, p1, k2.
Row 3 (inc): Kfb, k3, kfb (7 sts).
Row 4: K2, p3, k2.
Row 5 (inc): Kfb, k5, kfb (9 sts).
Row 6: K2, p5, k2.
Row 7 (inc): Kfb, k7, kfb (11 sts).
Row 8: K2, p7, k2.
Row 9 (inc): Kfb, k2, (p next st with sequin by bringing the yarn forwards, sliding the sequin to the work and purling the stitch, k1) 3 times, k1, kfb (13 sts).
Row 10: K2, p9, k2.
Row 11 (inc): Kfb, k11, kfb (15 sts).
Row 12: K2, p11, k2.
Row 13 (inc): Kfb, (k1, p next st with sequin) 6 times, k1, kfb (17 sts).
Row 14: K2, p13, k2.
Row 15 (inc): Kfb, k15, kfb (19 sts).
Row 16: K2, p15, k2.
Row 17 (inc): Kfb, k2, (p next st with sequin, k1) 7 times, k1, kfb (21 sts).
Row 18: K2, p17, k2.

child size only

Row 19: Knit.
Row 20: As row 18.
Break yarn and leave these sts on a holder.

adult size only

Row 19 (inc): Kfb, k19, kfb (23 sts).
Row 20: K2, p19, k2.
Row 21: K4, (p next st with sequin, k1) 8 times, k3.
Row 22: As row 20.
Break yarn and leave these sts on a holder.

second earflap

With 5mm needles and A, cast on 3 sts.
Work rows 1-20[22], as given for first earflap.

join earflaps

Row 1 (RS): Cast on and knit 6 sts, k3 sts from the second earflap, (p next st with sequin, k1) 8 times from the second earflap, k2, turn and cast on 27 sts, turn and k3 sts from the first earflap, (p next st with sequin, k1) 8 times from the first earflap, k2, turn and cast on 6 sts (81 sts).
Row 2 (WS): K8, p17, k31, p17, k8.
Row 3: Knit.
Row 4: As row 2.
Row 5: K8, (p next st with sequin, k1) 9 times, k30, (p next st with sequin, k1) 9 times, k7.
Row 6: Purl.
Row 7: Knit.
Row 8: Purl.
Row 9: K1, (p next st with sequin, k1) 13 times, k28, (p next st with sequin, k1) 13 times.
Rows 10-12: As rows 6-8.
Row 13: K2, (p next st with sequin, k1) 13 times, k26, (p next st with sequin, k1) 13 times, k1.
Rows 14-16: As rows 6-8.
Row 17: K1, (p next st with sequin, k1) 14 times, k24, (p next st with sequin, k1) 14 times.
Rows 18-20: As rows 6-8.
Row 21: K2, (p next st with sequin, k1) 14 times, k22, (p next st with sequin, k1) 14 times, k1.
Rows 22-24: As rows 6-8.
Row 25: K1, (p next st with sequin, k1) 40 times.
Rows 26-28: As rows 6-8.

shape crown

Row 29 (dec): K2tog, *(p next st with sequin, k1) 8 times, p next st with sequin, sl1, k2tog, psso; rep from * twice more, (p next st with sequin, k1) 8 times, p next st with sequin, k2togtbl (73 sts).
Row 30: Purl.
Row 31 (dec): K2tog, (k15, sl1, k2tog, psso) 3 times, k15, k2togtbl (65 sts).
Row 32: Purl.
Row 33 (dec): K2tog, k1, *(p next st with sequin, k1) 6 times, sl1, p2tog with sequin by bringing the yarn forwards, sliding the sequin to the work and purling the next 2 sts tog, psso, k1; rep from * twice more, (p next st with sequin, k1) 6 times, k2togtbl (57 sts).
Row 34: Purl.
Row 35 (dec): K2tog, (k11, sl1, k2tog, psso) 3 times, k11, k2togtbl (49 sts).
Row 36: Purl.
Row 37 (dec): K2tog, *(p next st with sequin, k1) 4 times, p next st with sequin, sl1, k2tog, psso; rep from * twice more, (p next st with sequin, k1) 4 times, p next st with sequin, k2togtbl (41 sts).
Row 38: Purl.
Row 39 (dec): K2tog, (k7, sl1, k2tog, psso) 3 times, k7, k2togtbl (33 sts).
Row 40: Purl.
Row 41 (dec): K2tog, k1, *(p next st with sequin, k1) twice, sl1, p2tog with sequin, psso, k1; rep from * twice more, (p next st with sequin, k1) twice, k2togtbl (25 sts).
Row 42: Purl.
Row 43 (dec): K2tog, (k3, sl1, k2tog, psso) 3 times, k3, k2togtbl (17 sts).
Break yarn and thread through rem sts, draw up tight and fasten off.

join earflaps

Row 1: Cast on and knit 6 sts, knit across 23 sts of second earflap, turn and cast on 27 sts, turn and knit across 23 sts of first earflap, turn and cast on 6 sts (85 sts).
Row 2 (WS): K8, p19, k31, p19, k8.
Row 3: K9, (p next st with sequin, k1) 9 times, k32, (p next st with sequin, k1) 9 times, k8.
Row 4: As row 2.
Row 5: Knit.
Row 6: Purl.
Row 7: K2, (p next st with sequin, k1) 13 times, k30, (p next st with sequin, k1) 13 times, k1.
Row 8: Purl.
Row 9: Knit.
Row 10: Purl.
Row 11: K1, (p next st with sequin, k1) 14 times, k28, (p next st with sequin, k1) 14 times.
Rows 12-14: As rows 8-10.
Row 15: K2, (p next st with sequin, k1) 14 times, k26, (p next st with sequin, k1) 14 times, k1.
Rows 16-18: As rows 8-10.
Row 19: K1, (p next st with sequin, k1) 15 times, k24, (p next st with sequin, k1) 15 times.
Rows 20-22: As rows 8-10.
Row 23: K2, (p next st with sequin, k1) 15 times, k22, (p next st with sequin, k1) 15 times, k1.
Rows 24-26: As rows 8-10.
Row 27: K1, (p next st with sequin, k1) 42 times.
Rows 28-30: As rows 8-10.
Row 31: K2, (p next st with sequin, k1) 41 times, k1.
Row 32: Purl.

shape crown

Row 33 (RS) (dec): K2tog, (k18, sl1, k2tog, psso) 3 times, k18, k2togtbl (77 sts).
Row 34 (WS): Purl.
Row 35 (dec): K2tog, *(p next st with sequin, k1) 8 times, sl1, p2tog with sequin by bringing the yarn forwards, sliding the sequin to the work and purling the next 2 sts tog, psso, (k1, p next st with sequin) 8 times**, sl1, k2tog, psso; rep from * to ** once more, k2togtbl (69 sts).
Row 36: Purl.
Row 37 (dec): K2tog, (k14, sl1, k2tog, psso) 3 times, k14, k2togtbl (61 sts).
Row 38: Purl.
Row 39 (dec): K2tog, *(k1, p next st with sequin) 6 times, sl1, k2tog, psso, (p next st with sequin, k1) 6 times**, sl1, p2tog with sequin, psso; rep from * to ** once more, k2togtbl (53 sts).
Row 40: Purl.
Row 41 (dec): K2tog, (k10, sl1, k2tog, psso) 3 times, k10, k2togtbl (45 sts).
Row 42: Purl.
Row 43 (dec): K2tog, *(p next st with sequin, k1) 4 times, sl1, p2tog with sequin, psso, (k1, p next st with sequin) 4 times**, sl1, k2tog, psso; rep from * to ** once more, k2togtbl (37 sts).
Row 44: Purl.
Row 45 (dec): K2tog, (k6, sl1, k2tog, psso) 3 times, k6, k2togtbl (29 sts).
Row 46: Purl.
Row 47 (dec): K2tog, *(k1, p next st with sequin) twice, sl1, k2tog, psso, (p next st with sequin, k1) twice**, sl1, p2tog with sequin, psso; rep from * to ** once more, k2togtbl (21 sts).
Row 48: Purl.
Row 49 (dec): K2tog, (k2, sl1, k2tog, psso) 3 times, k2, k2togtbl (13 sts).
Break yarn and thread through rem sts, draw up tight and fasten off.

earflap facing
(make 2)

Omit if you plan to add a knitted lining.
With 5mm needles and A, cast on 3 sts.
Row 1 (inc) (RS): Kfb, k1, kfb (5 sts).
Row 2 (WS): K2, p1, k2.
Row 3 (inc): Kfb, k3, kfb (7 sts).
Row 4: K2, p3, k2.
Row 5 (inc): Kfb, k5, kfb (9 sts).
Row 6: K2, p5, k2.
Row 7 (inc): Kfb, k7, kfb (11 sts).
Row 8: K2, p7, k2.
Row 9 (inc): Kfb, k9, kfb (13 sts).
Row 10: K2, p9, k2.
Row 11 (inc): Kfb, k11, kfb (15 sts).
Row 12: K2, p11, k2.
Row 13 (inc): Kfb, k13, kfb (17 sts).
Row 14: K2, p13, k2.
Row 15 (inc): Kfb, k15, kfb (19 sts).
Row 16: K2, p15, k2.
Row 17 (inc): Kfb, k17, kfb (21 sts).
Row 18: K2, p17, k2.

adult size only
Row 19 (inc): Kfb, k19, kfb (23 sts).
Row 20: K2, p19, k2.

both sizes
Next row: Knit.
Next row: As row 18[20].
Next: Rep the last 2 rows 3 more times.
Cast off loosely.

eyes *(make 2)*
Slip all stitches p-wise.

shape eyelid
With 3.25mm needles and B, cast on 14[16] sts.
Row 1 (RS): Purl.
Row 2 (WS): Sl1, k to last st, sl1.
Row 3: Purl.

eyeball
Join and cont in C.
Row 4 (WS): Sl1, p12[14], turn.
Row 5: Sl1, k11[13], turn.
Row 6: Sl1, p10[12], turn.
Row 7: Sl1, k9[11], turn.
Row 8: Sl1, p8[10], turn.
Row 9: Sl1, k7[9], turn.

adult size only
Row 10: Sl1, p8, turn.
Row 11: Sl1, k7, turn.

both sizes
Next row: Sl1, p7, pick up the horizontal loop before the next st and ptog with the next st to prevent a hole appearing in the work, turn.
Next row: Sl1, k8, pick up the horizontal loop before the next st and ktog with the next st, turn.
Next row: Sl1, p9, pick up the horizontal loop before the next st and ptog with the next st, turn.

adult size only
Next row: Sl1, k10, pick up the horizontal loop before the next st and ktog with the next st, turn.
Next row: Sl1, p11, pick up the horizontal loop before the next st and ptog with the next st, turn.

both sizes
shape lower edge of eye
Next row: Sl1, k10[12], change to yarn B, pick up the horizontal loop before the next st and ktog with the next st, turn. Cont with yarn B.
Next row: Sl1, p11[13], pick up the horizontal loop before the next st and ptog with the next st, turn.
Next row: Sl1, p12[14], pick up the horizontal loop before the next st and ptog with the next st, turn.
Cast off k-wise, leaving a long length of yarn B at the end.

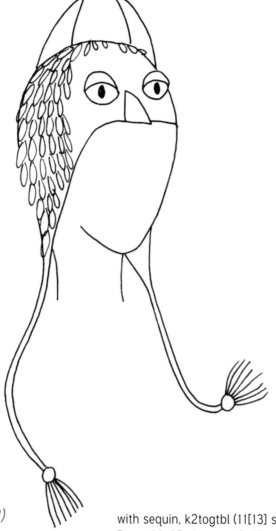

ears *(make 2)*
outer ear
Following the chart on page 95, and with 5mm needles and A, cast on 17[19] sts.

Rows 1-6: Starting with a k row, work 6 rows in st st.

Row 7: K2tog, (p next st with sequin, k1) 6[7] times, p next st with sequin, k2togtbl (15[17] sts).

Row 8: Purl.

Row 9: Knit.

Row 10: Purl.

Row 11 (dec): K2tog, (p next st with sequin, k1) 5[6] times, p next st with sequin, k2togtbl (13[15] sts).

Rows 12-14: As rows 8-10.

Row 15 (dec): K2tog, (p next st with sequin, k1) 4[5] times, p next st

with sequin, k2togtbl (11[13] sts).

Rows 16-18: As rows 8-10.

Row 19 (dec): K2tog, (p next st with sequin, k1) 3[4] times, p next st with sequin, k2togtbl (9[11] sts).

Rows 20-22: As rows 8-10.

Row 23 (dec): K2tog, (p next st with sequin, k1) 2[3] times, p next st with sequin, k2togtbl (7[9] sts).

Break yarn and thread through rem sts, draw up tight and fasten off.

inner ear
With 5mm needles and B, cast on 13[15] sts.

Rows 1-6: Starting with a k row, work 6 rows in st st.

Row 7: K2tog, k to last 2 sts, k2togtbl (11[13] sts).

Row 8: Purl.

Row 9: Knit.

Row 10: Purl.

Row 11 (dec): K2tog, k to last 2 sts, k2togtbl (9[11] sts).

Rows 12-14: As rows 8-10.

Row 15 (dec): K2tog, k to last 2 sts, k2togtbl (7[9] sts).

Rows 16-18: As rows 8-10.

Row 19 (dec): K2tog, k to last 2 sts, k2togtbl (5[7] sts).

Rows 20-22: As rows 8-10.

Row 23: Knit.

Break yarn and thread through rem sts, draw up tight and fasten off.

beak
With 3.25mm needles and B and D held together, cast on 19[23] sts.

Row 1 (RS): Knit.

Row 2 (WS): Purl.

Rows 3-4: As rows 1-2.

adult size only
Row 5 (dec): K10, sl1, k2tog, psso, k10 (21 sts).

Row 6 (dec): P9, sl1, p2tog, psso, p9 (19 sts).

both sizes
Next row (dec): K8, sl1, k2tog, psso, k8 (17 sts).

Next row (dec): P7, sl1, p2tog, psso, p7 (15 sts).

Next row (dec): K6, sl1, k2tog, psso, k6 (13 sts).

Next row (dec): P5, sl1, p2tog, psso, p5 (11 sts).

Next row (dec): K4, sl1, k2tog, psso, k4 (9 sts).

Next row (dec): P3, sl1, p2tog, psso, p3 (7 sts).

Next row (dec): K2, sl1, k2tog, psso, k2 (5 sts).

Break yarn and thread through rem sts, draw up tight and fasten off.

making up

Join the back seam with mattress stitch (see page 124). With RS together, sew the earflap facings, if applicable, to the earflaps, starting and finishing at the edge of the main section, leaving the overlapping cast-on edge open. Turn RS out and slip stitch the open edges to the inside of the main section.

beak

Stitch the side edges of the beak together and stuff firmly. Sew the beak to the centre front of the hat, just above the garter stitch edging, stitching all around the edge to attach it securely.

eyes

With the shaped eyelid at the top, sew each eye in place on either side of the beak and around $3/8$in (1cm) above the garter stitch edging. Stitch neatly around the edges, leaving an opening to insert a small amount of stuffing before closing. Sew a button to the centre of each eye.

ears

Stitch the inner ear to the outer ear, leaving the lower edge open. Add a thin layer of stuffing, keeping a flattened shape, and join the cast-off edges, so the inner ear is in the centre, with a slight overlap each side of the larger outer piece. To shape the ear, bring the two corners of each side of the lower edge together and stitch to hold in place. Sew the ears to the main section of the hat, stitching all around the lower edges to attach them securely.

finishing touches

If making a knitted lining, attach the twisted cords to the earflaps after joining the lining to the hat. Make two twisted cords (see page 126) using A, each measuring 8[12] in (20[30]cm) long, using 8[10] strands of yarn. Make two tassels (see page 127) measuring 4[5$1/8$]in (10[13]cm) long in B. Attach each to one end of the twisted cord, then stitch the other end of the cord to the tip of the earflap. Weave in all the yarn ends.

lining

See pages 130-138 for how to make and attach a cosy fleece or knitted lining.

child griffin hat

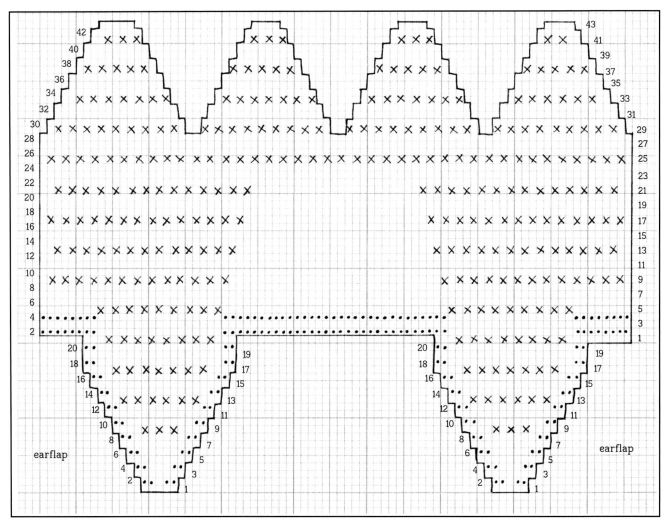

adult griffin hat

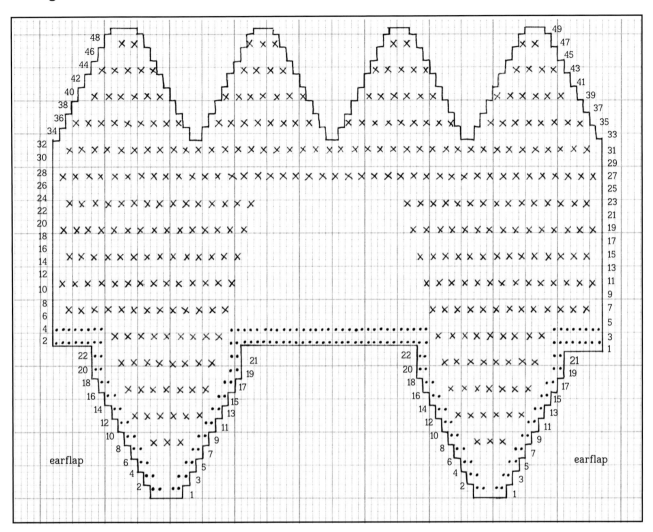

earflap

earflap

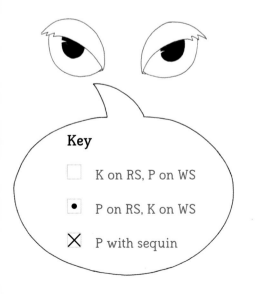

Key

☐ K on RS, P on WS

• P on RS, K on WS

☒ P with sequin

outer ear

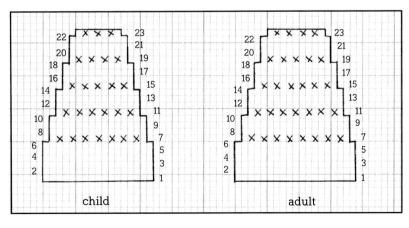

child

adult

This slouchy blob hat has a relaxed fit and features an all-over bobble pattern, a trio of eyes and bushy eyebrows, and a friendly smile.

Blob

materials

- King Cole Riot Chunky Tweed, 70% premium acrylic, 30% wool (145yd/134m per 100g ball):
  2[2] balls in 658 Moors (A)
- Oddment of DK yarn in white (B)
- Oddment of chunky yarn in black (C)
- 1 pair each of 4mm (UK8:US6), 6mm (UK4:US10) and 7mm (UK2:US10.5/11) knitting needles
- Small amount of toy stuffing
- 2 x 6in (15cm) long pipe cleaners
- Blunt-ended tapestry needle
- 3 x black ⅝in (1.5cm) diameter buttons
- Sewing needle
- Black thread

sizes

To fit: child, up to 20in (51cm) head circumference
[adult, up to 22in (56cm) head circumference]

tension

13 sts and 18 rows to 4in (10cm) over stocking stitch using 7mm needles. Use larger or smaller needles if necessary to obtain correct tension.

special abbreviation

MB: Make bobble

Knit into the front, back and front of the next stitch (three stitches made), turn and purl the three stitches, turn and knit into the front and back of all three stitches (six stitches made), do not turn, pass the second, third, fourth, fifth and sixth bobble stitches, one at a time, over the first bobble stitch (one stitch).

method

The hat is started with a k1, p1 rib and continues in a bobble pattern. The mouth is shaped by increasing stitches and is worked in reverse stocking stitch, with a few rows knitted between in stocking stitch to separate and define the top and bottom lips. The stitches of the eyes are decreased and the side edges of each piece are sewn together to form cup shapes that are stuffed so they pop out when stitched to the hat. The eyebrows are shaped by increasing stitches. The antennae are knitted strips covering pipe cleaners. These are topped with a knitted button. The lower ends are stuffed to help them stand up on the hat.

main section

With 6mm needles and A, cast on 60[64] sts.

rib
Row 1 (RS): (K1, p1) to end.
Rows 2-4: As row 1.

Change to 7mm needles. Continue in bobble pattern as follows:
Row 1 (RS) (inc): (Kfb, k9[7]) to end (66[72] sts).
Row 2 (WS): Purl.
Row 3: K3, (MB, k5) 10[11] times, MB, k2.
Row 4: Purl.
Row 5: Knit.
Row 6: Purl.
Row 7: Knit.
Row 8: Purl.
Row 9: (MB, k5) 11[12] times.
Rows 10-14: As rows 4-8.
Rep rows 3-14 2[3] more times.

child size only
Rep rows 3-9.

shape crown
Row 1 (WS) (dec): (P2tog, p4) 11 times (55 sts).
Row 2 (RS): Knit.
Row 3 (dec): (P2tog, p3) 11 times (44 sts).
Row 4: Knit.
Row 5 (dec): (P2tog, p2) 11 times (33 sts).
Row 6: K3, (MB, k5) 5 times.
Row 7 (dec): (P2tog, p1) 11 times (22 sts).
Row 8: Knit.
Row 9 (dec): (P2tog) 11 times (11 sts).
Break yarn and thread through rem sts, draw up tight and fasten off.

adult size only
Rep row 3.

shape crown
Row 1 (WS) (dec): (P2tog, p4) 12 times (60 sts).
Row 2 (RS): Knit.
Row 3 (dec): (P2tog, p3) 12 times (48 sts).
Row 4: Knit.
Row 5 (dec): (P2tog, p2) 12 times (36 sts).
Row 6: (MB, k5) 6 times.
Row 7 (dec): (P2tog, p1) 12 times (24 sts).
Row 8: Knit.
Row 9 (dec): (P2tog) 12 times (12 sts).
Break yarn and thread through rem sts, draw up tight and fasten off.

mouth

With 4mm needles and A, cast on 14[18] sts.
Row 1 (RS): Purl.
Row 2 (WS) (inc): Kfb, k to last st, kfb (16[20] sts).
Row 3: Purl.
Row 4 (inc): Kfb, k to last st, kfb (18[22] sts).
Rows 5-6: Purl.
Row 7 (inc): (Kfb, k1) 9[11] times (27[33] sts).
Rows 8-9: Purl.
Row 10 (inc): (Kfb, k2) 9[11] times (36[44] sts).
Row 11: Purl.
Row 12 (dec): (K2tog, k2) 9[11] times (27[33] sts).
Row 13: Purl.
Cast off, leaving a long length of yarn at the end.

eyes (make 3)
eye socket
With 4mm needles and A, cast on 15[20] sts.
Row 1 (RS): Purl.
Row 2 (WS): Knit.

eyeball
Join and cont in B.
Row 3: Knit.
Row 4: Purl.

adult size only
Row 5 (dec): (K2, k2tog) 5 times (15 sts).
Row 6: Purl.

both sizes
Next row (dec): (K1, k2tog) 5 times (10 sts).
Next row: Purl.
Break yarn and thread through rem sts, draw up to gather and fasten off, leaving a long length of A and B.

eyebrows (make 3)

With 4mm needles and C,
cast on 7[9] sts.
Row 1 (WS) (inc): (K1, kfb) 3[4]
times, k1 (10[13] sts).
Cast off p-wise, leaving a long
length of yarn at the end.

antennae (make 2)

With 4mm needles and A, cast on
12[15] sts.
Starting with a k row, work 5 rows
in st st.
Cast off k-wise, leaving a long
length of yarn at the end.

antennae tip

With 4mm needles and A,
cast on 7 sts.
Starting with a p row, work 11 rows
in rev st st, finishing on a RS row.
Cast off k-wise, leaving a long
length of yarn at the end.

making up

Join the back seam with mattress
stitch (see page 124).

mouth

Use the length of yarn left after
casting off to sew the mouth to
the hat above the ribbing, with the
cast-on edge at the top to form
a smile. Stitch neatly all around
the edges.

eyes

Use the lengths of A and B left after
fastening off to sew the side edges
of the eye together to form a cup
shape, matching the yarns. Sew the
eyes to the face, just above the
mouth, stitching carefully around
the outside edges and leaving
an opening to stuff them before
closing. Sew a button to each eye.

eyebrows

Use the lengths of yarn left after
casting off to sew the eyebrows to
the hat above the eyes, with the
cast-on stitches at the lower edge
so they are arched. Stitch all around
the edges to attach them.

antennae

Fold each pipe cleaner in half and
twist the two halves together. Turn
under the sharp edges and place
one twisted pipe cleaner in the
centre of the wrong side (purl side)
of each knitted strip. Fold the strip
around the pipe cleaner, bringing
the long edges together. Use the
length of yarn left after casting off
to sew the edges together, encasing
the pipe cleaner.
Sew together the cast-on and
cast-off edges of the tips of the
antennae to form a tube. Gather the
open edges at each end and work
a few stitches through the centre,
from one side to the other, to flatten
the piece, forming a button shape.
Stitch the knitted buttons to the
top of the antennae. Use the end
of a knitting needle to push a small
amount of stuffing firmly into the
first $^3/_4$in (2cm) of the open end of
each antenna. This will help them
to stand upright when attached to
the hat. Sew the antennae in place
above the eyebrows. Weave in all
the yarn ends.

lining

See pages 130–138 for how to
make and attach a cosy fleece
or knitted lining.

With its horrifying horns and ghastly gnashers, this skull hat is spectacularly spooky. Rather than knitting the details using the intarsia method, here the nasal aperture and teeth are embroidered onto the hat.

Skull

materials

- Wendy Mode Chunky, 50% wool, 50% acrylic (153yd/140m per 100g ball):

  1[1] ball in 220 Coal (A)

  1[1] ball in 202 Vanilla (B)

  1[1] ball in 254 Haze (C)

- 1 pair each of 4mm (UK8:US6), 6mm (UK4:US10) and 7mm (UK2:US10.5/11) knitting needles
- Small amount of toy stuffing
- Blunt-ended tapestry needle
- 2 x cream or white ⅞in (2.25cm) diameter buttons
- 2 x black ⅜in (1cm) diameter buttons
- Sewing needle
- Black thread

sizes

To fit: child, up to 20in (51cm) head circumference [adult, up to 22in (56cm) head circumference]

tension

13 sts and 18 rows to 4in (10cm) over stocking stitch using 7mm needles. Use larger or smaller needles if necessary to obtain correct tension.

method

The main part of the hat pattern is worked in the same format as the other projects, with a 2 x 1 rib replacing the earflaps. The coned shaping of the horns is formed by casting on stitches at the beginning of every alternate row. The curve is produced by increasing the stitches on the first half of the piece, then decreasing the stitches to finish the second half. The eye sockets are made by decreasing stitches and sewing the sides together to form discs. Buttons are stitched on to form the eyeballs, rolling around in the sockets. The nasal aperture and the teeth are embroidered in duplicate stitch, working over the knitted stitches.

main section

With 6mm needles and A, cast on 59[63] sts.
Row 1 (RS): K2[1], p1, (k2, p1) to last 2[1] st(s), k2[1].
Row 2 (WS): P2[1], k1, (p2, k1) to last 2[1] st(s), p2[1].
Rows 3-4: As rows 1-2.
Join and cont in B.
Change to 7mm needles.
Next row (RS) (inc): Kfb, k to last st, kfb (61[65] sts).
Starting with a purl row, work in st st for 17[19] rows, ending with a WS row.

shape crown

Row 1 (RS) (dec): K2tog, (k12[13], sl1, k2tog, psso) 3 times, k12[13], k2togtbl (53[57] sts).
Row 2 (WS): Purl.
Row 3 (dec): K2tog, (k10[11], sl1, k2tog, psso) 3 times, k10[11], k2togtbl (45[49] sts).
Row 4: Purl.

Row 5 (dec): K2tog, (k8[9], sl1, k2tog, psso) 3 times, k8[9], k2togtbl (37[41] sts).
Row 6: Purl.
Row 7 (dec): K2tog, (k6[7], sl1, k2tog, psso) 3 times, k6[7], k2togtbl (29[33] sts).
Row 8: Purl.
Row 9 (dec): K2tog, (k4[5], sl1, k2tog, psso) 3 times, k4[5], k2togtbl (21[25] sts).
Row 10: Purl.
Row 11 (dec): K2tog, (k2[3], sl1, k2tog, psso) 3 times, k2[3], k2togtbl (13[17] sts).

adult size only

Row 12: Purl.
Row 13 (dec): K2tog, (k1, sl1, k2tog, psso) 3 times, k1, k2togtbl (9 sts).

both sizes

Break yarn and thread through rem sts, draw up tight and fasten off.

eye sockets (make 2)

With 4mm needles and A, cast on 25 sts.
Row 1 (RS) (dec): (K2, k2tog) 6 times, k1 (19 sts).
Row 2 (WS): Purl.
Row 3 (dec): (K1, k2tog) 6 times, k1 (13 sts).
Break yarn and thread through rem sts, draw up to gather and fasten off.

horns (make 2)

With 4mm needles and C, cast on 2 sts.
Row 1 (RS) (inc): Knit.
Row 2 (WS): P1, sl1 p-wise.
Row 3 (inc): Cast on and knit 2 sts, kfb, k1 (5 sts).
Row 4: P to last st, sl1 p-wise.

Row 5 (inc): Cast on and knit 2 sts, kfb, k1, kfb, k2 (9 sts).
Row 6: P to last st, sl1 p-wise.
Row 7 (inc): Cast on and knit 2 sts, kfb, k1, kfb, k2, kfb, k3 (14 sts).
Row 8: P to last st, sl1 p-wise.
Row 9 (inc): Cast on and knit 2 sts, kfb, k1, kfb, k2, kfb, k3, kfb, k4 (20 sts).
Row 10: P to last st, sl1 p-wise.
Row 11 (inc): Cast on and knit 2 sts, kfb, k1, kfb, k2, kfb, k3, kfb, k4, kfb, k5 (27 sts).
Row 12: P to last st, sl1 p-wise.
Row 13 (inc): Cast on and knit 2 sts, kfb, k1, kfb, k2, kfb, k3, kfb, k4, kfb, k5, kfb, k6 (35 sts).
Row 14: P to last st, sl1 p-wise.
Row 15 (inc): Cast on and knit 2 sts, kfb, k1, kfb, k2, kfb, k3, kfb, k4, kfb, k5, kfb, k6, kfb, k7 (44 sts).

child size only

Row 16: P to end.
Row 17 (inc): (K2, kfb) twice, k3, kfb, k4, kfb, k5, kfb, k6, kfb, k7, kfb, k8 (51 sts).
Row 18: Purl.
Row 19 (dec): (K2, k2togtbl) twice, k3, k2togtbl, k4, k2togtbl, k5, k2togtbl, k6, k2togtbl, k7, k2togtbl, k8 (44 sts).

adult size only

Row 16: P to last st, sl1 p-wise.
Row 17 (inc): Cast on and knit 2, kfb, k1, kfb, k2, kfb, k3, kfb, k4, kfb, k5, kfb, k6, kfb, k7, kfb, k8 (54 sts).
Row 18: P to end.
Row 19 (inc): (K2, kfb) twice, k3, kfb, k4, kfb, k5, kfb, k6, kfb, k7, kfb, k8, kfb, k9 (62 sts).
Row 20: Purl.
Row 21 (dec): (K2, k2togtbl) twice, k3, k2togtbl, k4, k2togtbl, k5, k2togtbl, k6, k2togtbl, k7, k2togtbl, k8, k2togtbl, k9 (54 sts).

Row 22: P to last st, sl1 p-wise.
Row 23 (dec): Cast off 3 sts, (k2, k2togtbl) twice, k3, k2togtbl, k4, k2togtbl, k5, k2togtbl, k6, k2togtbl, k7, k2togtbl, k8 (44 sts).

both sizes
Next row: P to last st, sl1 p-wise.
Next row (dec): Cast off 3 sts, (k2, k2togtbl) twice, k3, k2togtbl, k4, k2togtbl, k5, k2togtbl, k6, k2togtbl, k7 (35 sts).
Next row: P to last st, sl1 p-wise.
Next row (dec): Cast off 3 sts, (k2, k2togtbl) twice, k3, k2togtbl, k4, k2togtbl, k5, k2togtbl, k6 (27 sts).
Next row: P to last st, sl1 p-wise.
Next row (dec): Cast off 3 sts, (k2, k2togtbl) twice, k3, k2togtbl, k4, k2togtbl, k5 (20 sts).
Next row: P to last st, sl1 p-wise.
Next row (dec): Cast off 3 sts, (k2, k2togtbl) twice, k3, k2togtbl, k4 (14 sts).
Next row: P to last st, sl1 p-wise.
Next row (dec): Cast off 3 sts, (k2, k2togtbl) twice, k3 (9 sts).
Next row: P to last st, sl1 p-wise.

Next row (dec): Cast off 3 sts, k2, k2togtbl, k2 (5 sts).
Next row: P to last st, sl1 p-wise.
Next row (dec): Cast off 3 sts, k2 (2 sts).
Next row: P1, sl1 p-wise.
Cast off, leaving a long length of yarn at the end.

making up
Join the back seam with mattress stitch (see page 124).

teeth and nasal aperture
Use the duplicate stitch technique (see page 129) and yarn B to embroider six teeth on the central knit stitches of the ribbing, working over two columns of four rows of rib and two cast-on stitches at the lower edge to form each tooth. Using yarn A, embroider the nasal hole in duplicate stitch, 3 stitches wide and 3[4] rows high, beginning each side of the hole around $5/8$ [$3/4$]in (1.5[2]cm) from the rib and starting the centre stitches one row above (see chart below).

eyes
Sew the side edges together to form a disc. Stitch eyes to the hat, sewing all around the outer edges. Place a black button over a larger cream or white button and sew to the centre of each eye socket.

horns
Sew the side edges of the horns together, matching the shaping. Stuff them firmly. Sew a horn to each side of the hat, just below the top, stitching all around the lower edges to attach them securely. Curl the narrow end up and secure with a few stitches through the horn. Weave in all the yarn ends.

lining
See pages 130–138 for how to make and attach a fleece or knitted lining.

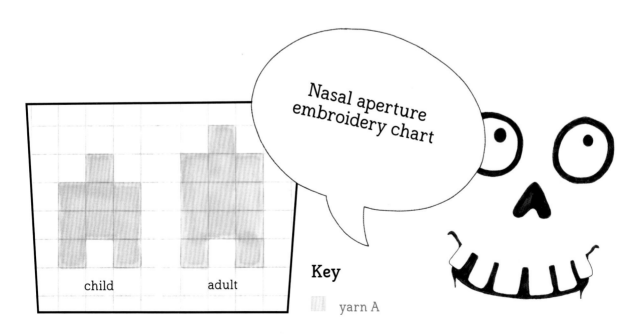

Nasal aperture embroidery chart

child   adult

Key

yarn A

Troll

This troll features big ears, mismatched eyes and a bulbous nose. The tufty strands of hair are curly knitted I-cords.

materials

- Sirdar Hayfield Chunky Tweed, 74% acrylic, 20% wool, 6% viscose (158yd/145m per 100g ball):
  1[1] ball in 0189 Malvern (A)
- Sirdar Bоufflé, 42% cotton, 33% acrylic, 15% wool, 10% nylon (109yd/100m per 50g ball):
  1[1] ball in 0721 Verde (B)
- Oddment of DK yarn in white (C)
- 1 pair each of 4mm (UK8:US6), 6mm (UK4:US10) and 7mm (UK2:US10.5/11) knitting needles
- 1 pair of 4mm (UK8:US6) double-pointed needles
- Small amount of toy stuffing
- Blunt-ended tapestry needle
- Stranded embroidery thread in black
- Embroidery needle
- 2 x black ⅝in (1.5cm) diameter buttons
- Sewing needle
- Black thread

sizes

To fit: child, up to 20in (51cm) head circumference [adult, up to 22in (56cm) head circumference]

tension

13 sts and 18 rows to 4in (10cm) over stocking stitch using 7mm needles. Use larger or smaller needles if necessary to obtain correct tension.

method

The hat is started with a 2 x 2 rib and then continued in stocking stitch. The ears are knitted in stocking stitch and shaped by increasing and decreasing the stitches. The side and lower edges are joined and the corners at the base of the ears are stitched together before sewing them to the hat. The shaping of the nose is done by increasing the central stitches, then the last two rows at the end of the nose are decreased. The side edges are sewn together and the nose is stuffed to form a teardrop shape and finished with embroidered nostrils. The eyes are different sizes; both are started with the outer edges, knitted in reverse stocking stitch. The yarn is changed to make the eyeball, which is continued in stocking stitch. The side edges are joined to form a shallow cup that is stuffed to make the eye pop out of the hat. Buttons are stitched on to finish the eyes and I-cord tufts of hair are stitched to the top of the hat.

main section

With 6mm needles and A, cast on 60[64] sts.

child size only
Row 1 (RS): P1, (k2, p2) to last 3 sts, k2, p1.
Row 2 (WS): K1, (p2, k2) to last 3 sts, p2, k1.
Rows 3-4: As rows 1-2.

adult size only
Row 1 (RS): K1, (p2, k2) to last 3 sts, p2, k1.
Row 2 (WS): P1, (k2, p2) to last 3 sts, k2, p1.
Rows 3-4: As rows 1-2.

both sizes
Change to 7mm needles.
Next row (RS) (inc): Kfb, k to end (61[65] sts).
Starting with a purl row, work in st st for 17[19] rows, ending with a WS row.

shape crown
Row 1 (RS) (dec): K2tog, (k12[13], sl1, k2tog, psso) 3 times, k12[13], k2togtbl (53[57] sts).
Row 2 (WS): Purl.
Row 3 (dec): K2tog, (k10[11], sl1, k2tog, psso) 3 times, k10[11], k2togtbl (45[49] sts).
Row 4: Purl.
Row 5 (dec): K2tog, (k8[9], sl1, k2tog, psso) 3 times, k8[9], k2togtbl (37[41] sts).
Row 6: Purl.
Row 7 (dec): K2tog, (k6[7], sl1, k2tog, psso) 3 times, k6[7], k2togtbl (29[33] sts).
Row 8: Purl.
Row 9 (dec): K2tog, (k4[5], sl1, k2tog, psso) 3 times, k4[5], k2togtbl (21[25] sts).
Row 10: Purl.

Row 11 (dec): K2tog, (k2[3], sl1, k2tog, psso) 3 times, k2[3], k2togtbl (13[17] sts).

adult size only
Row 12: Purl.
Row 13 (dec): K2tog, (k1, sl1, k2tog, psso) 3 times, k1, k2togtbl (9 sts).

both sizes
Break yarn and thread through rem sts, draw up tight and fasten off.

tufts of hair *(make 3)*

With 4mm double-pointed needles and B, cast on 3 sts.
Row 1: Knit 3, do not turn, slide the sts along the needle to the other end so the length of yarn is attached to the last st on the needle.
Row 2: K1, pulling the yarn taut so as not to leave a gap in the work, sl1, k1, do not turn, slide the sts along the needle to the other end of the needle.
Row 3: As row 2.
This will produce the curly I-cord. Rep rows 1-3 until the cord measures 2½[3]in (6.5[7.5]cm) unstretched. Slide the sts along the needle to the other end and cast off, leaving a long length of yarn at the end.

ears *(make 2)*

Starting at the tip of the ear, with 6mm needles and A, cast on 6 sts.
Row 1 (WS): Purl.
Row 2 (RS) (inc): Kfb, k1, (kfb) twice, k1, kfb (10 sts).
Row 3: Purl.
Row 4 (inc): Kfb, k3, (kfb) twice, k3, kfb (14 sts).

Row 5: Purl.
Row 6 (inc): Kfb, k5, (kfb) twice, k5, kfb (18 sts).
Row 7: Purl.
Row 8 (inc): Kfb, k7, (kfb) twice, k7 kfb (22 sts).
Row 9: Purl.
Row 10 (inc): Kfb, k9, (kfb) twice, k9, kfb (26 sts).
Row 11: Purl.
Row 12 (inc): Kfb, k11, (kfb) twice, k11, kfb (30 sts).

adult size only
Row 13: Purl.
Row 14 (inc): Kfb, k13, (kfb) twice, k13, kfb (34 sts).

both sizes
Work 7[9] rows in st st, ending with a WS row.
Next row (RS) (dec): (K2tog) 15[17] times (15[17] sts).
Cast off k-wise.

eyes

child size – small eye

With 4mm needles and A, cast on 24 sts.

Row 1 (RS): Purl.
Row 2: Knit.
Row 3: Purl.
Join and cont in C.
Row 4 (WS): Purl.
Row 5 (dec): (K2tog, k1) 8 times (16 sts).
Row 6: Purl.
Row 7 (dec): (K2tog) 8 times (8 sts).
Row 8: Purl.
Break yarn, leaving a long length of each, and thread C through rem sts, draw up tight and fasten off.

child size – large eye & adult size – small eye

With 4mm needles and A, cast on 30 sts.

Row 1 (RS): Purl.
Row 2: Knit.
Row 3: Purl.
Join and cont in C.
Row 4 (WS): Purl.
Row 5 (dec): (K2tog, k1) 10 times (20 sts).
Row 6: Purl.
Row 7 (dec): (K2tog) 10 times (10 sts).
Row 8: Purl.
Break yarn, leaving a long length of each, and thread C through rem sts, draw up tight and fasten off.

adult size – large eye

With 4mm needles and A, cast on 35 sts.

Row 1 (RS): Purl.
Row 2 (WS): Knit.
Row 3: Purl.
Join and cont in C.
Row 4: Purl.
Row 5 (dec): (K2tog, k3) 7 times (28 sts).
Row 6: Purl.

Row 7 (dec): (K2tog) 14 times (14 sts).
Row 8: Purl.
Break yarn, leaving a long length of each, and thread C through rem sts, draw up tight and fasten off.

nose

With 4mm needles and A, cast on 6 sts.

Row 1 (RS) (inc): K2, (kfb) twice, k2 (8 sts).
Row 2 (WS): Purl.
Row 3 (inc): K3, (kfb) twice, k3 (10 sts).
Row 4: Purl.
Row 5 (inc): K4, (kfb) twice, k4 (12 sts).
Row 6: Purl.
Row 7 (inc): K5, (kfb) twice, k5 (14 sts).
Row 8: Purl.
Row 9 (inc): K6, (kfb) twice, k6 (16 sts).
Row 10: Purl.

adult size only

Row 11 (inc): K7, (kfb) twice, k7 (18 sts).
Row 12: Purl.
Row 13 (inc): K8, (kfb) twice, k8 (20 sts).
Row 14: Purl.

both sizes

Next row (RS) (dec): (K2tog) 8[10] times (8[10] sts).
Next row (dec): (P2tog) 4[5] times (4[5] sts).
Break yarn, leaving a long length and thread through rem sts, draw up tight and fasten off.

making up

Join the back seam with mattress stitch (see page 124).

tufts of hair

With the length of yarn left after fastening off, sew the tufts of hair to the top of the hat.

ears

Fold the ear and sew the side edges together. Stitch the cast-off edges together. To shape the ear, bring the two corners of each side of the lower edge to the middle and stitch to hold the shaping in place. Sew the ears to the main section of the hat, stitching all around the edges to attach them securely.

nose

Sew together the side edges of the nose, leaving an opening to stuff before closing to form a teardrop shape. With the seam at the back, sew the nose to the centre front of the hat, so the wide end just overhangs the rib. Work a few stitches through each side of the nose into the hat to hold it in place. Embroider nostrils in satin stitch (see page 129), using three strands of embroidery thread.

eyes

Use the lengths of A and C left after fastening off to sew the side edges of the eye together to form a cup shape, matching the colours. Sew the eyes to the face on each side of the nose, stitching carefully around the outside edges and leaving an opening to stuff them before closing. Sew a button to each eye. Weave in all the yarn ends.

lining

See pages 130–138 for how to make and attach a cosy fleece or knitted lining.

OTHER THINGS YOU NEED TO KNOW

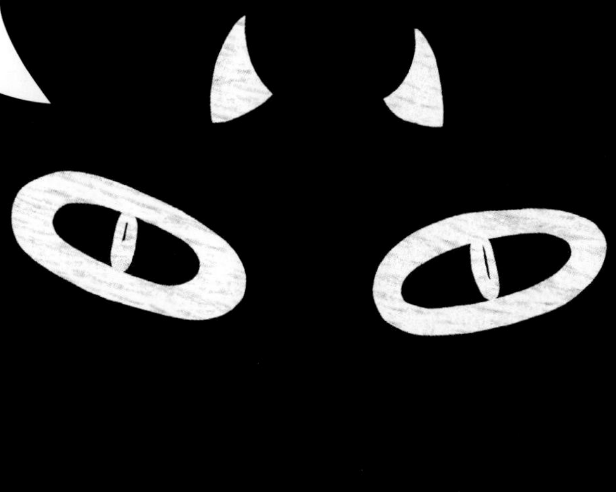

Getting started

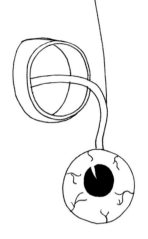

A list of the materials required to make each hat can be found at the beginning of the pattern. This allows you to gather together the right size needles and amount of yarn required, as well as any other necessary items, before you begin.

Sizing

The finished monster hats are intended to fit children up to 20in (51cm) head circumference, and adults up to 22in (56cm) head circumference.

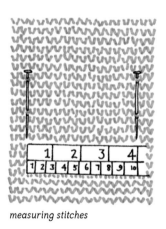

measuring stitches

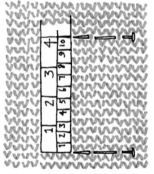

measuring rows

Tension

Checking the tension before starting a project is vital, as this will affect the size and look of the finished piece. The tension is the number of rows and stitches per square inch or centimetre of knitted fabric. Using the same needles and stitch that the tension has been measured over in the pattern, knit a sample of around 5in (12.5cm) square and then smooth it out on a flat surface.

Stitches

To measure the tension of stitches, place a ruler horizontally across the work and mark 4in (10cm) with pins. Count the number of stitches between the pins, including half stitches. This will give you the tension of the stitches.

Rows

Measure the tension of rows by placing a ruler vertically over the work and mark 4in (10cm) with pins. Count the number of rows between the pins. If the number of stitches and rows is greater than those stated in the pattern, your tension is tighter and you should use larger needles. If the number of stitches and rows is fewer than those stated in the pattern, your tension is looser, so you should use smaller needles.

Knitting needles

Single-pointed straight knitting needles come in pairs. They are used throughout this book for making the monster hats. Circular needles have a flexible nylon cord joining two straight needles and are used for knitting both flat and tubular pieces. They are ideal for working on large projects that require a longer needle. Double-pointed needles are used for knitting in the round to produce seamless tubes of fabric. Knitting needles are available in a variety of sizes and materials, such as bamboo, metal, plastic and wood. Using larger or smaller sized needles will change the look of the fabric and will also affect the tension and the amount of yarn required.

Tapestry needles

A blunt-ended tapestry needle is used to sew the projects together. The rounded end will prevent any snagging, while the large eye makes it easy to thread the needle with the thicker yarns.

Substituting yarns

When substituting yarns, it is important to calculate the number of balls required by the number of yards or metres per ball rather than the weight of the yarn, as this varies according to the fibre.

Tension is also important. Always work a tension swatch in the yarn you wish to use before starting a project.

Reading patterns

The monster hat patterns are written for children's and adults' sizes. The children's size is given first; where the adult's instructions differ, the adjustment is given inside the square [ ] brackets. If 0 appears in the instructions, then no stitches or rows are to be worked for this size. Where there is no bracket after the stitches or rows given, the instructions refer to both sizes.

Reading charts

Each square of a chart represents one stitch and each horizontal row represents one row of knitting. The changes of colour or pattern are shown as actual colour or symbols.

Read the chart from the bottom row to the top, working from right to left for right-side rows and from left to right for wrong-side rows.

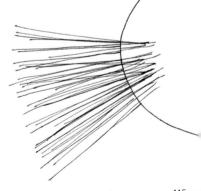

Knitting basics

Here, the knitting basics are explained, including casting on and casting off, knitting the stitches, shaping the knitted fabric and sewing the seams.

Slip knot

The first stitch on the needle is the slip knot or loop.

1   Take the end of the yarn and form it into a ring. Insert the needle through the ring, catching the long end that is attached to the ball, and draw it back through.

2   Keeping the yarn looped on the needle, pull through until the loop closes around the needle, ensuring it is not tight. Pulling on the long end of yarn will loosen the knot, whereas pulling on the short end will tighten it.

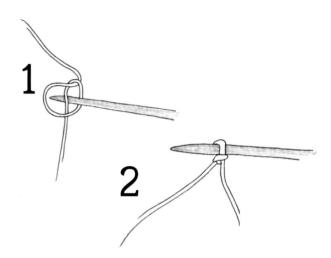

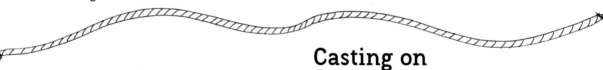

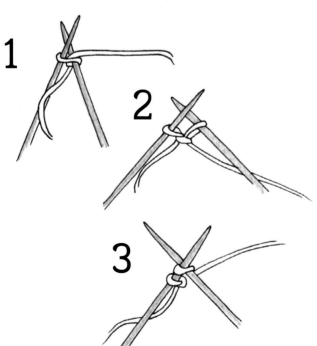

Casting on

The first step is to cast on. There are several methods for this. Each produces a different edge and can be chosen according to the desired finish. Two techniques use both knitting needles; the third uses just one.

Cast on

This method is worked through the stitch, producing a loose edge that can be tightened by working into the backs of the stitches on the first row.

1   With the slip knot on the left-hand needle, insert the right-hand needle and pass the yarn under and over the point.

2   Pull the loop just made through the stitch.

3   Pass the loop onto the left-hand needle.

Repeat the last three steps until the required number of stitches has been made.

Cable cast on

This produces a corded foundation row, suitable for items that require an elastic but firm edge.

1-3 Work steps 1-3 of the basic cast-on method to make the first two stitches.
4   For the third and following stitches, insert the right-hand needle between the two stitches on the left-hand needle, pass the yarn around the point of the right-hand needle to make a loop and pull through to the front of the work. Pass the loop onto the left-hand needle.

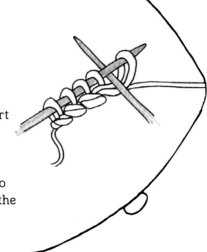

Thumb method

This edge is worked towards the end of the yarn rather than the ball as in the previous methods, so you need to allow enough length at the beginning.

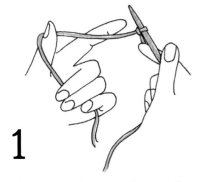

1

Make a slip knot on the needle, leaving a long length of yarn. Hold the needle in your right hand. With the length of yarn in the left hand, pass it around the left thumb and hold in place with the fingers.

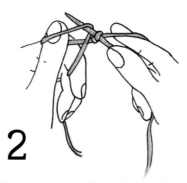

2

Insert the needle under and up through the loop on the thumb.

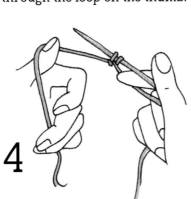

4

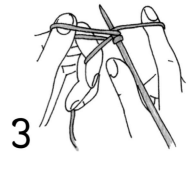

3

With the right hand, pass the yarn from the ball up and over the point of the needle.

Draw the yarn through the loop on the thumb, forming the new stitch on the needle. Remove the thumb from the loop and pull on the end of the yarn to tighten the stitch.

Knit stitch

This stitch creates a reversible fabric of garter stitch when worked on every row. Each stitch is worked from the left-hand needle to the right-hand needle to form a row of knitting. Then the needles are swapped to the opposite hands to begin another row.

1

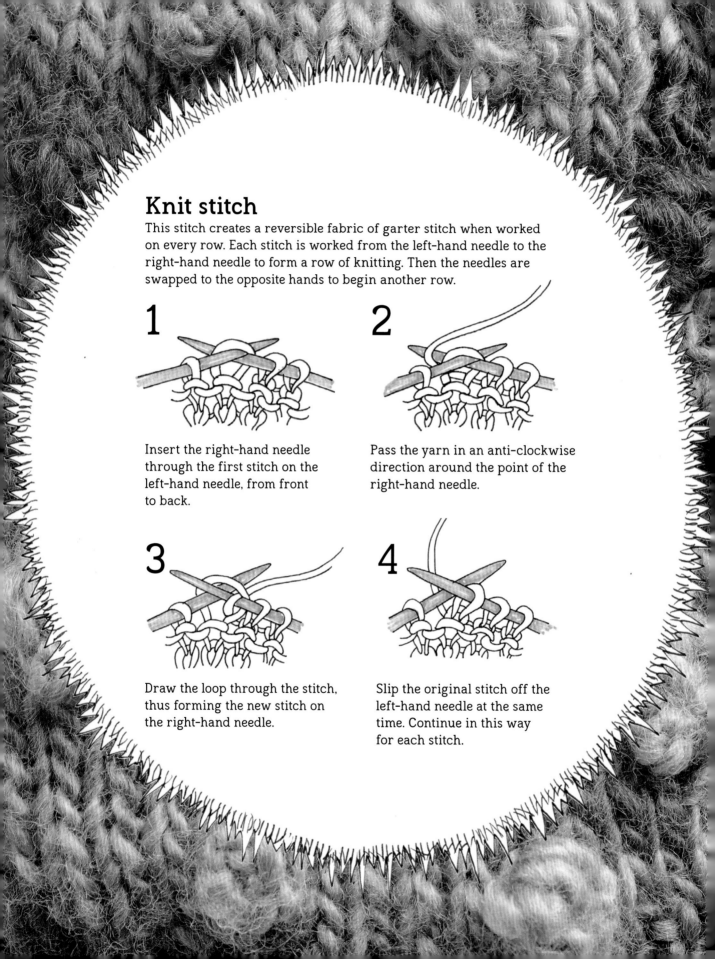

Insert the right-hand needle through the first stitch on the left-hand needle, from front to back.

2

Pass the yarn in an anti-clockwise direction around the point of the right-hand needle.

3

Draw the loop through the stitch, thus forming the new stitch on the right-hand needle.

4

Slip the original stitch off the left-hand needle at the same time. Continue in this way for each stitch.

Purl stitch

The purl stitch is the reverse of the knit stitch. The stitch on the left-hand needle is slipped off to the front of the work. If the purl stitch is used on every row, the effect will be the same as the knit stitch, creating a garter stitch fabric. By alternating rows of knit and purl, stocking stitch fabric is produced. A rib stitch is formed by alternating knit and purl stitches.

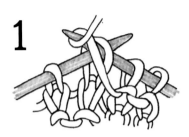

1
With the yarn at the front of the work, insert the right-hand needle through the first stitch, from back to front. Pass the yarn in an anti-clockwise direction around the point of the right-hand needle.

2
Draw the loop through the stitch, forming the new stitch on the right-hand needle.

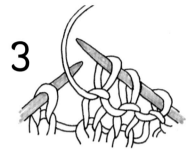

3
Slip the original stitch off the left-hand needle at the same time. Continue in this way for each stitch.

Garter stitch

Knit every row.

Stocking stitch

Row 1 (RS): Knit.
Row 2 (WS): Purl.
Repeat rows 1 and 2 to form stocking stitch.

Reverse stocking stitch

This is the reverse side of the stocking stitch, where the purl rows are on the right side of the fabric.
Row 1 (RS): Purl.
Row 2 (WS): Knit.
Repeat rows 1 and 2 to form reverse stocking stitch.

Knitting into the front or back loop of a stitch

The front of a stitch is the loop that is closer to you. This is the loop that is generally knitted into. The back loop of the stitch is the one further away.

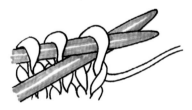

knitting into front loop

To knit into the front loop, insert the needle from left to right into the next stitch.

knitting into back loop

To knit into the back loop, insert the needle from right to left, into the back of the next stitch.

Increasing

1

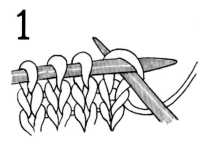

To increase (kfb), insert the right-hand needle knitwise into the next stitch, pass the yarn around the right needle and pull it through, but leave the original stitch on the needle.

2

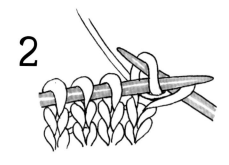

Insert the right needle into the back of the same stitch, pass the yarn around the needle, pull it through and slip the original stitch off the needle. You will now have two stitches on the needle.

Decreasing

Knitwise

To decrease knitwise (k2tog), insert the needle, from front to back, into the next two stitches on the left-hand needle, pass the yarn around the right-hand needle, then draw the loop through the two stitches, slipping them off the needle at the same time. This will slant the stitches towards the right on the knit side of the work.

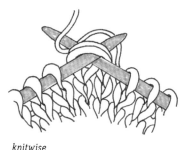

knitwise

Purlwise

To decrease purlwise (p2tog), insert the needle, from back to front, into the next two stitches on the left-hand needle, pass the yarn around the right-hand needle, then draw the loop through the two stitches, slipping them off the needle at the same time. This will slant the stitches towards the right on the knit side of the work.

purlwise

K2togtbl

To knit two stitches together through the back loops of the stitches, insert the needle from right to left, through the back of the next two stitches and knit together. This will slant the stitches towards the left on the knit side of the work.

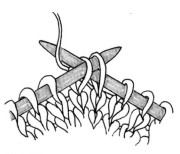

K2togtbl

Make loop (ML)

In steps 1 and 2, the yarn is wound in a figure-of-eight direction to create two loops on the right-hand needle. The yarn that has been wound around the finger creates the finished loop of the Zombie's hair on page 74.

1

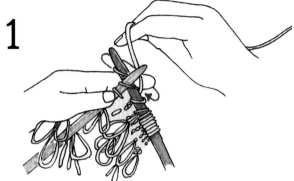

Insert the right-hand needle into the next stitch. With the left forefinger under the right-hand needle, wind the yarn in a clockwise direction over the right-hand needle and forefinger once.

2

Wind the yarn around just the needle as usual and knit the stitch, keeping the forefinger in the loop.

3

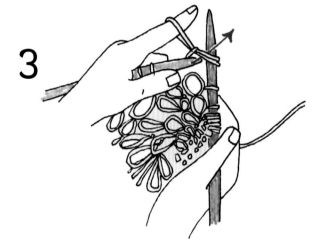

Slip both loops just made back onto the left-hand needle and knit them together through the back loops.

4

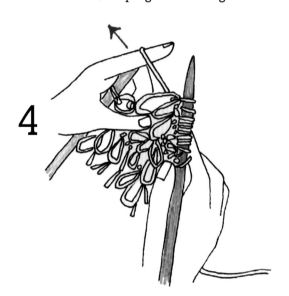

Remove finger from loop. Ensure that the loop is at the front of the work before commencing with the next stitch.

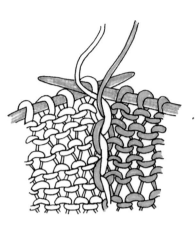

Intarsia

The intarsia technique uses blocks of colour to create a design. It is used for the Yeti hat on page 69. Use small balls of yarn for each area of colour and twist them as they meet at the back of the work, rather than carrying them across the entire row; this will prevent tangling and keep the stitches neat.

Cast off

Casting off is important to keep the stitches from unravelling and to create a neat edge. It is important not to cast off too tightly so the work has some elasticity.

Cast off knitwise

1

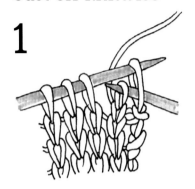

Knit two stitches. Insert the point of the left-hand needle into the first stitch worked and pass it over the second stitch and off the right-hand needle.

2

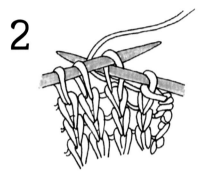

One stitch is now on the right-hand needle. Knit the next stitch so there are two stitches on the right-hand needle, then pass the first stitch over the second and off the needle as before. Repeat until there is just one stitch remaining. Break the yarn and draw through the last stitch to fasten off.

Cast off purlwise
To cast off in purl, repeat as for knitwise, working in purl stitch instead of knit.

Seams

Seams should be joined using a blunt-ended tapestry needle and matching yarn — preferably a long length that has been left at the beginning or end of the work, as it is already fastened in place. If you are joining in new yarn to sew the pieces together, leave a length at the beginning that can be darned in afterwards to avoid any untidy ends showing. Make sure any pattern or shaping is matched.

Mattress stitch

The mattress stitch produces an invisible seam that is suitable for stocking stitch fabric. It produces a neat finish, ideal for joining the seam at the back of the hats.

Place the two edges to be joined side by side with the right sides of the work facing you. Insert the needle under the horizontal bar between the first two stitches on one side, then under the same bar on the other piece. Continue picking up the stitches and drawing the edges together, every few stitches, to join the seam.

Edge-to-edge seam

This method is particularly suitable if you wish to avoid a bulky seam. It is perfect for joining delicate articles as well as creating a flat seam with elasticity. Place the two pieces of work together with the edges meeting and the right sides facing you. Join the seam by picking up a loop from the edge of each side alternately. Do not pull the stitches too tight.

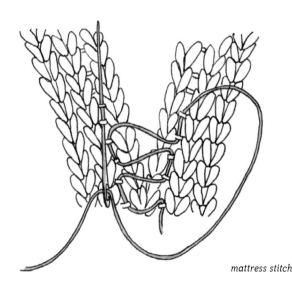

mattress stitch

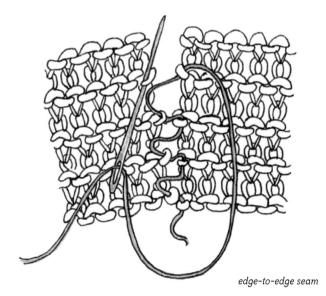

edge-to-edge seam

Back-stitch seam

For this type of seam, it is important to work your stitches neatly and in a straight line.

1   With right sides together and working one stitch in from the edge, begin by working a couple of stitches over each other to secure. Bring the needle through to the front of the work one stitch ahead of the last stitch.

2   Insert the needle back through the work at the end of the previous stitch, then bring the needle up to the front, one stitch ahead of the one just made. Continue to complete the seam.

1

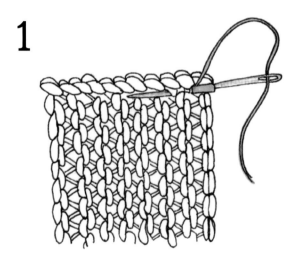

2

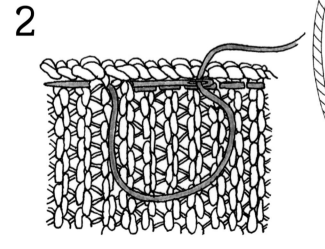

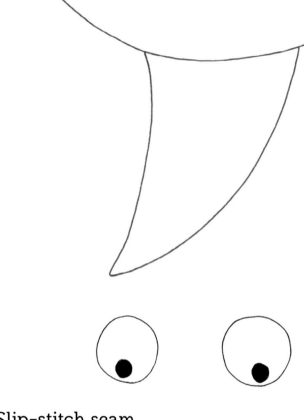

Slip-stitch seam

Insert the needle into a stitch on the wrong side of the knitting and then into a stitch on the cast-on or cast-off edge. Repeat to the end, keeping the stitches even and not too tight.

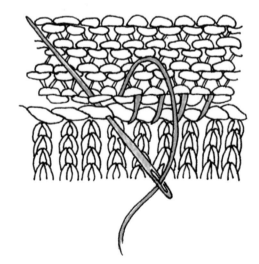

Finishing touches

Small embroidered features or large colourful tassels swinging jauntily from woolly cords are used to create interesting additional details that turn perfectly ordinary knitted hats into something altogether more spooky. Here is how to add those extra decorations that make the monsters come to life.

Twisted cord

1 Measure around ⁷/₈[1¹/₃]yd (0.8[1.2]m) lengths of the required number of strands of yarn stated in the pattern. This will give you extra length to sew and weave the ends into the earflaps. Knot the ends of the yarn together. Slip one end over a coat hook and insert a pencil into the other end. Hold the pencil between your thumb and forefinger, keeping the yarn taut. Turn the pencil clockwise to twist the strands.

2 Continue turning the pencil until the strands are tightly twisted. Fold them, allowing the two halves to twist together naturally. Remove the pencil and carefully undo the knots. With a strand threaded onto a needle, wind the yarn around the cord near the top and secure with a few stitches. Alternatively, the end can be knotted but it will be bulkier.

Striped cord

1 Measure around ⁷/₈[1¹/₃]yd (0.8[1.2]m) lengths of half the total required number of strands of yarn stated in the pattern in each of two colours. This will give you extra length to sew and weave the ends into the earflaps. Fold the lengths of one colour in half and knot the ends together to form a loop of stranded yarn. Thread the strands of the remaining colour through the loop and knot those ends together. Slip the knotted end of one loop over a coat hook and insert a pencil through the other loop. Hold the pencil between your thumb and forefinger, keeping the yarn taut. The point where the yarn is intertwined should be in the middle.

2 Turn the pencil clockwise until the strands are tightly twisted. Fold them in the middle, where the two colours meet and allow them to twist together naturally, producing a striped effect. Finish as for the twisted cord.

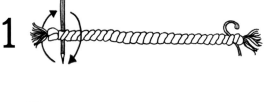

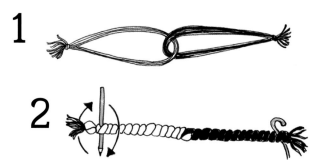

Tassels

1   Cut a piece of card to the required length of the finished tassel. Wind the yarn around the card to the desired thickness. Break yarn, leaving a long length and thread it through a needle. Slip the needle through all the loops on the card and tie the yarn tightly at the top edge.

2   Remove the card and wind the yarn around the loops, a little way down from the tied top end, securing with a few stitches and drawing the needle through to the top to leave an end to stitch to the cord. Cut through the folded lower edge and trim to neaten the ends.

1

2

Embroidery stitches

These simple stitches are used to add features to many of the hats, including Fiery, Zombie and Skull on pages 36, 72 and 102.

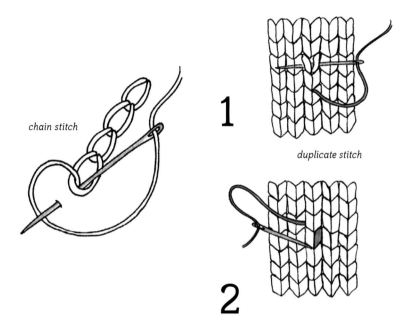

chain stitch

1

duplicate stitch

2

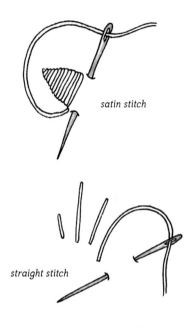

satin stitch

straight stitch

Chain stitch

Bring the yarn through to the right side of the work at the position where the stitch is to be made and hold it down with your left thumb. Insert the needle where it first came out and bring it back through a little way from the last point, according to the length of the stitch you wish to make. Pull through, keeping the yarn under the needle. Repeat to continue the chain.

Duplicate stitch

1 Insert the needle from the back to the front of the work at the base of the 'V' formed by the knitted stitch that you want to embroider over. At the front of the work, insert your needle behind both arms of the stitch above it and pull the yarn through.

2 Insert the needle back through the point where it first emerged to cover the knitted stitch.

Satin stitch

Work straight stitches side by side and close together across a shape. Take care to keep the stitches even and the edge neat. The finished result will look like satin.

Straight stitch

This is a single stitch that can be worked in varying lengths. It is useful for embroidering short lines.

Fleece linings

Add a lining to your monster hat to make it even cosier.
Choose a fabric with some stretch that feels soft to the touch,
in a contrasting or a matching colour.

Fabric lining materials

- 22 x 22in (56 x 56cm) [25 x 25in (63.5 x 63.5cm)] of stretch fabric, such as polar fleece or jersey
- Matching thread
- Needle
- Dressmaking pins
- Squared pattern paper
- Pencil
- Scissors

Method

1   Scale the pattern template to size, transferring all the markings onto the paper. Cut out the pattern, following the continuous line. Seam allowances of ⅝in (1.5cm) are included in the pattern. Place the pattern on the folded fabric, ensuring that the fold indicated on the pattern is placed exactly on the fold of the fabric. Pin the pattern in position and cut out the fabric.

2   Stitch the darts indicated on the pattern template. Cut to within ½in (1.25cm) of the point of the dart and press open. With right sides together, pin and stitch the main seam, allowing for a ⅝in (1.5cm) seam. Trim the seam and cut notches in the curve, taking care not to cut into the stitching.

3   Turn under the hem and pin the lining to the inside of the hat, just above the knitted edging or the ribbing, with the main seam of the lining at the centre back of the hat. Ease the fabric evenly around the lower edge. Slip stitch in place by hand. Work a few stitches through the top of the crown into the knitted hat to keep the lining in place.

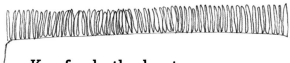

Key for both charts

1 square = ⅜in (1cm)
⅝in (2.5cm) seam allowance is included

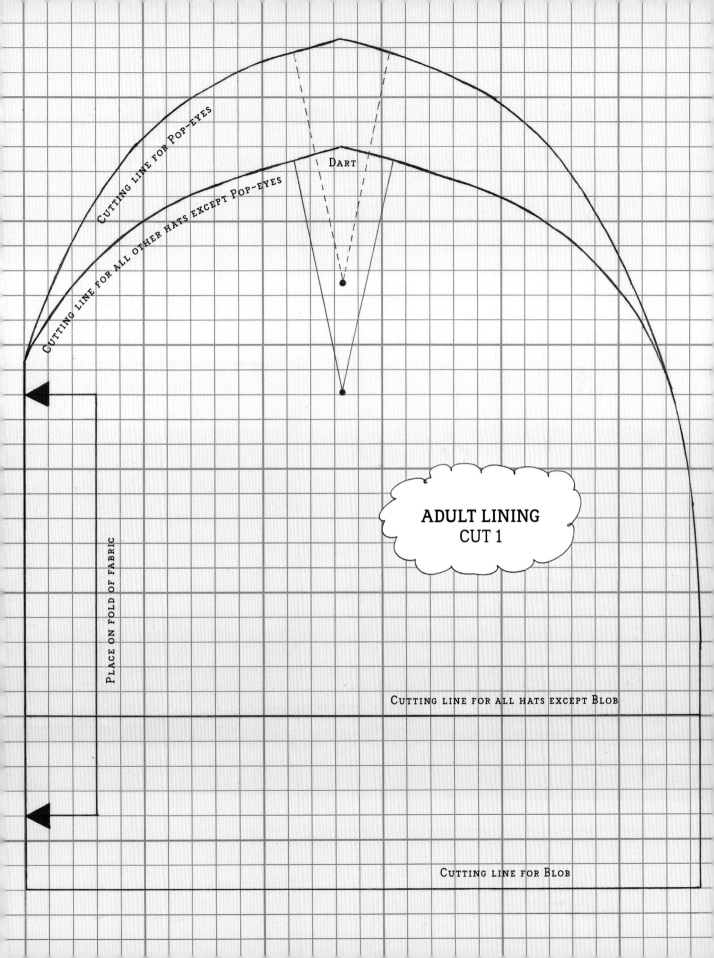

CUTTING LINE FOR POP-EYES

CUTTING LINE FOR ALL OTHER HATS EXCEPT POP-EYES

DART

PLACE ON FOLD OF FABRIC

ADULT LINING
CUT 1

CUTTING LINE FOR ALL HATS EXCEPT BLOB

CUTTING LINE FOR BLOB

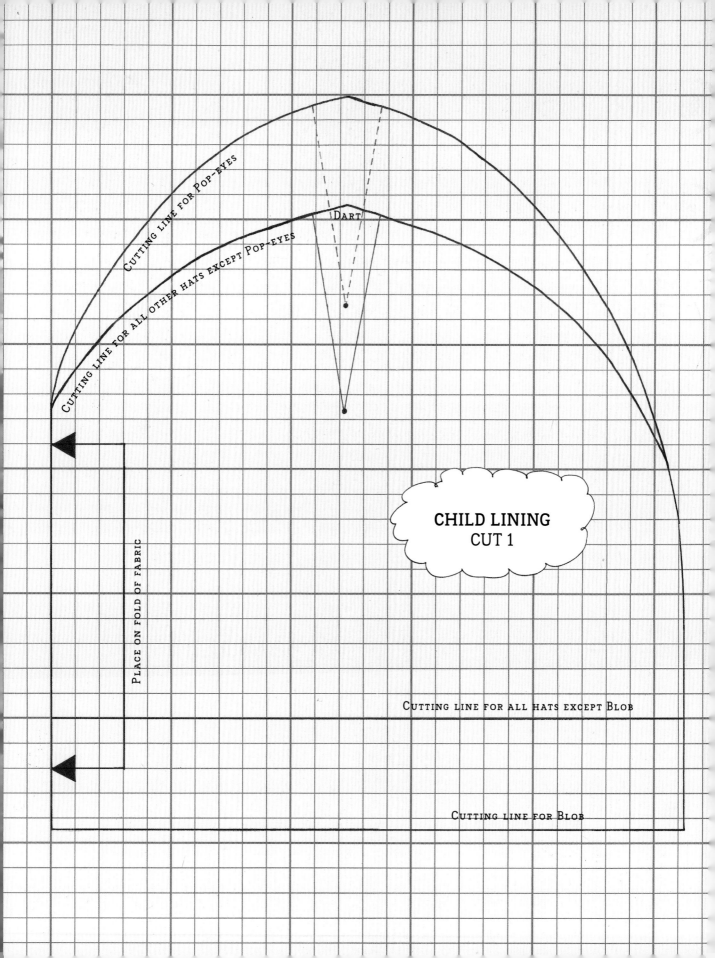

Cutting line for Pop-eyes

Cutting line for all other hats except Pop-eyes

Dart

Place on fold of fabric

CHILD LINING
CUT 1

Cutting line for all hats except Blob

Cutting line for Blob

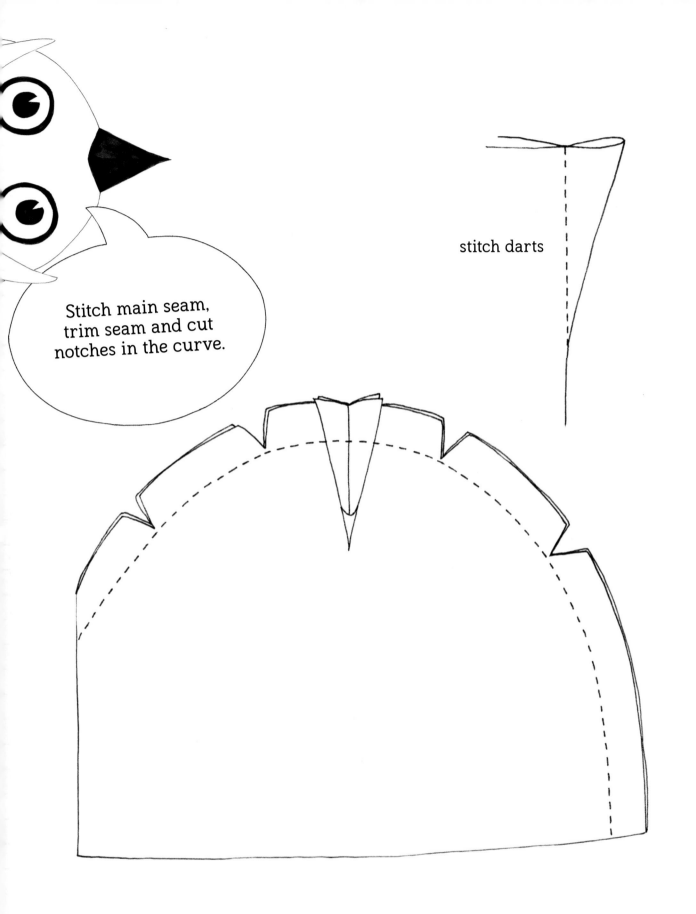

Knitted linings

A knitted lining is a cosy alternative to the fleece lining. It can be worked in the same shade as the monster hat, or you can choose a contrast colour. As the earflap facings are worked into the knitted lining pattern, omit them where applicable from the pattern when knitting the hat. The lining is stitched in place after the features are added to the main part of the hat. If twisted cords are to be attached to the earflaps, the knitted lining should go in first.

materials

- ⚪ Approximately 50g yarn for Pop-eyes; 100g yarn for other monster hats (A)
- ⚪ See chosen monster hat pattern for required needle sizes
- ⚪ Stitch holder
- ⚪ Blunt-ended tapestry needle

sizes

To fit: child, up to 20in (51cm) head circumference [adult, up to 22in (56cm) head circumference]

tension

See chosen monster hat pattern for required tension.

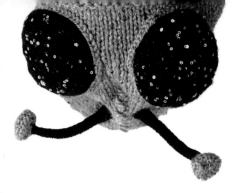

method

The knitted lining is worked in the same yarn as the hat you are making: refer to the pattern for the yarn type, needles required and tension. The earflap facings are worked first, where applicable. The main part of the lining is then continued in stocking stitch. The back seam is joined and the lining slipped inside the hat and stitched in place. Then finish with twisted cords and tassels, if using.

Cyclops, Demon, Fly, Fang and Yeti
first earflap facing

*Using yarn A and 6.5mm needles for Fang and Yeti, 7mm needles for Fly and Cyclops or 8mm needles for Demon, cast on 3 sts.
Row 1 (inc) (RS): Kfb, k1, kfb (5 sts).
Row 2: K2, p1, k2.
Row 3 (inc): Kfb, k3, kfb (7 sts).
Row 4: K2, p3, k2.
Row 5 (inc): Kfb, k5, kfb (9 sts).
Row 6: K2, p5, k2.
Row 7 (inc): Kfb, k7, kfb (11 sts).
Row 8: K2, p7, k2.
Row 9 (inc): Kfb, k9, kfb (13 sts).
Row 10: K2, p9, k2.
Row 11 (inc): Kfb, k11, kfb (15 sts).
Row 12: K2, p11, k2.

adult size only
Row 13 (inc): Kfb, k13, kfb (17 sts).
Row 14: K2, p13, k2.

both sizes
Next row: Knit.
Next row: As row 12[14].*
Break yarn and leave these sts on a holder.

second earflap facing
Work as given for first earflap from * to *.
Next row: Cast on and knit 5 sts, knit across 15[17] sts of second earflap, turn, cast on 21 sts, turn, knit across 15[17] sts of first earflap, turn, cast on 5 sts (61[65] sts).
Next row (WS): K7, p11[13], k25, p11[13], k7.
Next row: Knit.
Rep last 2 rows once more and then starting with a p row, work 19[21] rows in st st, ending with a WS row.

shape crown
Row 1 (RS) (dec): K2tog, (k12[13], sl1, k2tog, psso) 3 times, k12[13], k2tog (53[57] sts).
Row 2: Purl.
Row 3 (dec): K2tog, (k10[11], sl1, k2tog, psso) 3 times, k10[11], k2tog (45[49] sts).

Row 4: Purl.
Row 5 (dec): K2tog, (k8[9], sl1, k2tog, psso) 3 times, k8[9], k2tog (37[41] sts).
Row 6: Purl.
Row 7 (dec): K2tog, (k6[7], sl1, k2tog, psso) 3 times, k6[7], k2tog (29[33] sts).
Row 8: Purl.
Row 9 (dec): K2tog, (k4[5], sl1, k2tog, psso) 3 times, k4[5], k2tog (21[25] sts).
Row 10: Purl.
Row 11 (dec): K2tog, (k2[3], sl1, k2tog, psso) 3 times, k2[3], k2tog (13[17] sts).

adult size only
Row 12: Purl.
Row 13 (dec): K2tog, (k1, sl1, k2tog, psso) 3 times, k1, k2tog (9 sts).

both sizes
Break yarn and thread through rem sts, draw up tight and fasten off.

Alien, Fluffball, Skull, Slug, Troll and Zombie

Using A and 8mm needles for Fluffball or 7mm needles for Alien, Skull, Slug, Troll and Zombie, cast on 61[65] sts.
Starting with a knit row, work in st st for 18[20] rows, ending with a WS row.

shape crown

Work as for Cyclops, Demon, Fly, Fang and Yeti.

Blob

Using 7mm needles and A, cast on 66[72] sts.
Starting with a knit row, work in st st for 44[50] rows, ending with a WS row.

shape crown

Row 1 (RS) (dec): (K2tog, k4) 11[12] times (55[60] sts).
Row 2 (WS): Purl.
Row 3 (dec): (K2tog, k3) 11[12] times (44[48] sts).
Row 4: Purl.
Row 5 (dec): (K2tog, k2) 11[12] times (33[36] sts).
Row 6: Purl.
Row 7 (dec): (K2tog, k1) 11[12] times (22[24] sts).
Row 8: Purl.
Row 9 (dec): (K2tog) 11[12] times (11[12] sts).
Break yarn and thread through rem sts, draw up tight and fasten off.

Griffin and Fiery

first earflap facing

*With 5mm needles and A, cast on 3 sts.
Row 1 (inc) (RS): Kfb, k1, kfb (5 sts).
Row 2 (WS): K2, p1, k2.
Row 3 (inc): Kfb, k3, kfb (7 sts).
Row 4: K2, p3, k2.
Row 5 (inc): Kfb, k5, kfb (9 sts).
Row 6: K2, p5, k2.
Row 7 (inc): Kfb, k7, kfb (11 sts).
Row 8: K2, p7, k2.
Row 9 (inc): Kfb, k9, kfb (13 sts).
Row 10: K2, p9, k2.
Row 11 (inc): Kfb, k11, kfb (15 sts).
Row 12: K2, p11, k2.
Row 13 (inc): Kfb, k13, kfb (17 sts).
Row 14: K2, p13, k2.
Row 15 (inc): Kfb, k15, kfb (19 sts).
Row 16: K2, p15, k2.
Row 17 (inc): Kfb, k17, kfb (21 sts).
Row 18: K2, p17, k2.

adult size only

Row 19 (inc): Kfb, k19, kfb (23 sts).
Row 20: K2, p19, k2.

both sizes

Next row: Knit.
Next row: As row 18[20].*
Break yarn and leave these sts on a holder.

second earflap facing

Work as given for first earflap from * to *.
Next row: Cast on and knit 6 sts, knit across 21[23] sts of second earflap, turn and cast on 27 sts, turn and knit across 21[23] sts of first earflap, turn and cast on 6 sts (81[85] sts).
Next row (WS): K8, p17[19], k31, p17[19], k8.

Next row: Knit.
Rep last 2 rows once more.
Starting with a purl row, work 23[27] rows in st st.

shape crown

Row 1 (dec): K2tog, (k17[18], sl1, k2tog, psso) 3 times, k17[18], k2togtbl (73[77] sts).
Row 2: Purl.
Row 3 (dec): K2tog, (k15[16] sl1, k2tog, psso) 3 times, k15[16], k2togtbl (65[69] sts).
Row 4: Purl.
Row 5 (dec): K2tog, (k13[14], sl1, k2tog, psso) 3 times, k13[14], k2togtbl (57[61] sts).
Row 6: Purl.
Row 7 (dec): K2tog, (k11[12], sl1, k2tog, psso) 3 times, k11[12], k2togtbl (49[53] sts).
Row 8: Purl.
Row 9 (dec): K2tog, (k9[10], sl1, k2tog, psso) 3 times, k9[10], k2togtbl (41[45] sts).
Row 10: Purl.
Row 11 (dec): K2tog, (k7[8], sl1, k2tog, psso) 3 times, k7[8], k2togtbl (33[37] sts).
Row 12: Purl.
Row 13 (dec): K2tog, (k5[6], sl1, k2tog, psso) 3 times, k5[6], k2togtbl (25[29] sts).
Row 14: Purl.
Row 15 (dec): K2tog, (k3[4], sl1, k2tog, psso) 3 times, k3[4], k2togtbl (17[21] sts).
Break yarn and thread through rem sts, draw up tight and fasten off.

Pop-eyes

first earflap facing

*With 5mm needles and A, cast on 3 sts.
Row 1 (inc) (RS): Kfb, k1, kfb (5 sts).
Row 2 (WS): K2, p1, k2.
Row 3 (inc): Kfb, k3, kfb (7 sts).
Row 4: K2, p3, k2.
Row 5 (inc): Kfb, k5, kfb (9 sts).
Row 6: K2, p5, k2.
Row 7 (inc): Kfb, k7, kfb (11 sts).
Row 8: K2, p7, k2.
Row 9 (inc): Kfb, k9, kfb (13 sts).
Row 10: K2, p9, k2.
Row 11 (inc): Kfb, k11, kfb (15 sts).
Row 12: K2, p11, k2.
Row 13 (inc): Kfb, k13, kfb (17 sts).
Row 14: K2, p13, k2.
Row 15 (inc): Kfb, k15, kfb (19 sts).
Row 16: K2, p15, k2.
Row 17 (inc): Kfb, k17, kfb (21 sts).
Row 18: K2, p17, k2.

adult size only

Row 19 (inc): Kfb, k19, kfb (23 sts).
Row 20: K2, p19, k2.

both sizes

Next row: Knit.
Next row: As row 18[20].*
Break yarn and leave these sts on a holder.

second earflap facing

Work as given for first earflap from * to *.
Next row: Cast on and knit 6 sts, knit across 21[23] sts of second earflap, turn and cast on 27 sts, turn and knit across 21[23] sts of first earflap, turn and cast on 6 sts (81[85] sts).

Next row (WS): K8, p17[19], k31, p17[19], k8.
Next row: Knit.
Rep last 2 rows once more. Starting with a purl row, work 23[27] rows in st st.

shape crown

Row 1 (dec): K2tog, (k17[18], sl1, k2tog, psso) 3 times, k17[18], k2togtbl (73[77] sts).
Row 2: Purl.
Row 3: Knit.
Row 4: Purl.
Row 5 (dec): K2tog, (k15[16] sl1, k2tog, psso) 3 times, k15[16], k2togtbl (65[69] sts).
Row 6: Purl.
Row 7: Knit.
Row 8: Purl.
Row 9 (dec): K2tog, (k13[14], sl1, k2tog, psso) 3 times, k13[14], k2togtbl (57[61] sts).
Row 10: Purl.
Row 11: Knit.
Row 12: Purl.
Row 13 (dec): K2tog, (k11[12], sl1, k2tog, psso) 3 times, k11[12], k2togtbl (49[53] sts).
Row 14: Purl.
Row 15: Knit.
Row 16: Purl.
Row 17 (dec): K2tog, (k9[10], sl1, k2tog, psso) 3 times, k9[10], k2togtbl (41[45] sts).
Row 18: Purl.
Row 19: Knit.

Row 20: Purl.
Row 21 (dec): K2tog, (k7[8], sl1, k2tog, psso) 3 times, k7[8], k2togtbl (33[37] sts).
Row 22: Purl.
Row 23: Knit.
Row 24: Purl.
Row 25 (dec): K2tog, (k5[6], sl1, k2tog, psso) 3 times, k5[6], k2togtbl (25[29] sts).
Row 26: Purl.
Row 27: Knit.
Row 28: Purl.
Row 29 (dec): K2tog, (k3[4], sl1, k2tog, psso) 3 times, k3[4], k2togtbl (17[21] sts).
Break yarn and thread through rem sts, draw up tight and fasten off.

making up

Join the back seam with mattress stitch (see page 124). With WS together, pin the lining in place inside the main part of the hat and slip stitch neatly around the lower edges. For the Alien, Blob, Fluffball, Skull, Troll and Zombie, slip stitch the lower edge of the lining to the first row of stocking stitch after the rib on the main part, or after the garter stitch edging if making the Slug. Work a few stitches into the top of the crown to stop the lining slipping.

Knitting needle sizes

UK	Metric	US
11	3mm	–
10	3.25mm	3
–	3.5mm	4
9	3.75mm	5
8	4mm	6
7	4.5mm	7
6	5mm	8
5	5.5mm	9
4	6mm	10
3	6.5mm	10$\frac{1}{2}$
2	7mm	10$\frac{3}{4}$
0	8mm	11
00	9mm	13

Abbreviations

cm	centimetres
cont	continue
dec	decrease
in	inch(es)
inc	increase
k	knit
k-wise	knitwise
kfb	knit into the front and back of the same stitch to increase
k2tog	knit 2 stitches together to decrease
k2togtbl	knit 2 stitches together through the back loops to decrease
m	metres
mm	millimetres
p	purl
p2tog	purl 2 stitches together to decrease
patt	pattern
psso	pass slipped stitch over
p-wise	purlwise
rem	remain(ing)
rep	repeat
rev st st	reverse stocking stitch
RS	right side
sl	slip
st(s)	stitch(es)
st st	stocking stitch
WS	wrong side
yd	yards
yfd	yarn forward

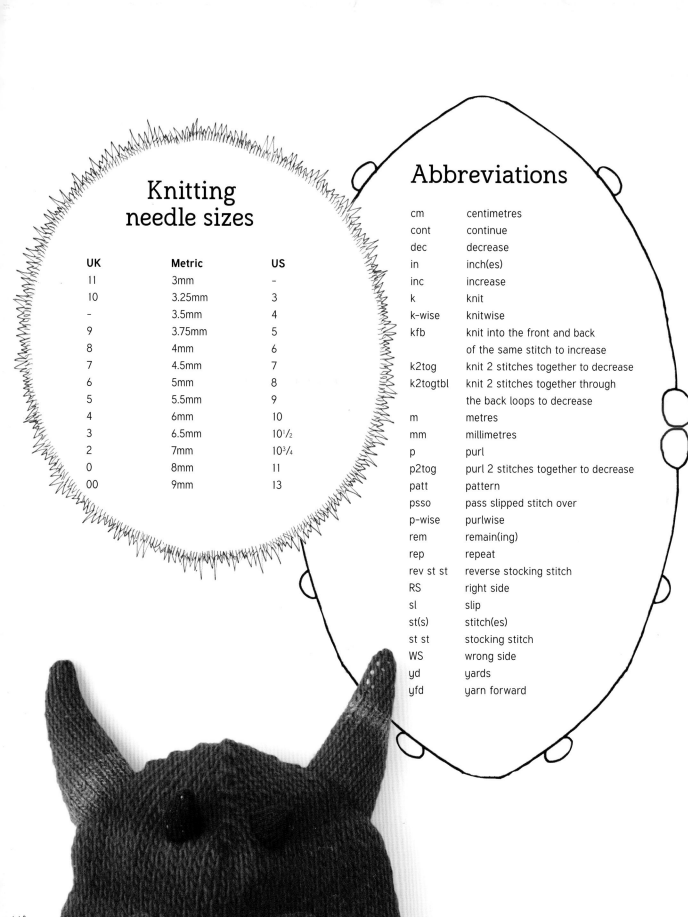

Thank you very much to Jonathan Bailey for giving me the opportunity to write *Monster Hats*. Thank you to Wendy McAngus for all her support and to everyone at GMC. I would like to thank my family: my husband, Damian; my children, Miriam, Dilys, Flynn and Honey; and my grandchildren, Dolly, Leo and Winter. They have all been very patient, modelling the hats and giving me endless encouragement throughout the process of creating the monsters.

The publishers would like to thank our models Isobel Robson at MOT models, Ruari Allardyce and Flynn Mooncie. Make up was by Jen Dodson.

Thank you

Suppliers

YARN AND NEEDLES

Germany
Rico Design
Industriestrasse 19-23
33034 Brakel
Tel: +49 (0)52 726020
www.rico-design.de

Norway
Drops Design
Jerikoveien 10 A
1067 Oslo
Tel: +47(0) 2330 3220
www.garnstudio.com

UK
Deramores
Unit 8 Conqueror Court
Watermark Business Park
Sittingbourne, Kent
ME10 5BH
Tel: 0845 519 4573
www.deramores.com

King Cole Ltd
Merrie Mills
Snaygill Industrial Estate
Keighley Road, Skipton,
North Yorkshire
BD23 2QR
Tel: +44 (0)1756 703670
www.kingcole.co.uk

Loveknitting Ltd
6th Floor, Corinthian House
279 Tottenham Court Road
London, W1T 7RJ
Tel: 0845 544 2196
www.loveknitting.com

Sirdar Spinning Ltd
Flanshaw Lane
Wakefield
West Yorkshire
WF2 9ND
Tel: +44 (0)1924 371501
www.sirdar.co.uk

Stylecraft
PO Box 62
Goulbourne Street
Keighley, West Yorkshire
BD21 1PP
Tel: +44 (0)1535 609798
www.stylecraft-yarns.co.uk

The Stitchery
12-16 Riverside, Cliffe Bridge
High Street, Lewes
East Sussex, BN7 2RE
Tel: +44 (0)1273 473577
www.the-stitchery.co.uk

Wool Warehouse
12 Longfield Road
Sydenham Industrial Estate
Leamington Spa,
Warwickshire, CV31 1XB
Tel: +44 (0)1926 882818
www.woolwarehouse.co.uk

USA
Brooklyn General Store
128 Union Street, Brooklyn
NY 11231
Tel: +1 718 237 7753
www.brooklyngeneral.com

Lion Brand Yarn
135 Kero Road
Carlstadt, NJ 07072
Tel: +1 800 661 7551
www.lionbrand.com

Purl Soho
459 Broome Street
New York, NY 10013
Tel: +1 212 420 8796
www.purlsoho.com

BUTTONS

UK
The Button Company
41 Terminus Road, Chichester,
West Sussex, PO19 8TX
Tel: +44 (0)1243 775462
www.buttoncompany.co.uk

Wool Warehouse
(see Yarn and Needles)

EMBROIDERY THREADS AND NEEDLES

UK
DMC
DMC Creative World Ltd
Unit 21, Warren Park Way
Warrens Park, Enderby
Leicester, LE19 4SA
Tel: +44 (0)116 2754000
www.dmccreative.co.uk

Willow Fabrics
95 Town Lane
Mobberley
Knutsford
Cheshire WA16 7HH
Tel: +44 (0)1565 872225
www.willowfabrics.com

USA
Purl Soho
(see Yarn and Needles)

Brooklyn General Store
(see Yarn and Needles)

SEQUINS

UK
Simply Sequins Limited
82 Durrants Road
Rowlands Castle
Hants
PO9 6BG
Tel: +44 (0)239 2476125
www.simplysequins.co.uk

WADDING AND TOY STUFFING

UK
Deramores
(see Yarn and Needles)

Hobbycraft
Customer Services
E-Commerce Door A
Parkway
Centrum 100 Business Park,
Unit 1
Burton Upon Trent
DE14 2WA
Tel: +44 (0)330 0261400
www.hobbycraft.co.uk

Loveknitting Ltd
(see Yarn and Needles)

Wold of Wool
Unit 8
The Old Railway Goods Yard
Scar Lane
Milnsbridge
Huddersfield
West Yorkshire
HD3 4PE
Tel: +44 (0)1484 846878
www.worldofwool.co.uk

USA
Purl Soho
(see Yarn and Needles)

Index

WWW.GMCBOOKS.COM

To place an order, or to request a catalogue, contact: GMC Publications Ltd,
Castle Place, 166 High Street, Lewes, East Sussex,
BN7 1XU, United Kingdom. Tel: +44 (0)1273 488005